ONE SQUARE MILE

A HISTORY OF TRENTON
JUNCTION, NEW JERSEY

MARK W. FALZINI

ONE SQUARE MILE
A HISTORY OF TRENTON JUNCTION, NEW JERSEY

iUniverse books may be ordered through booksellers or by contacting:

iUniverse
1663 Liberty Drive
Bloomington, IN 47403
www.iuniverse.com
1-800-Authors (1-800-288-4677)

ISBN: 978-1-5320-1750-6 (sc)
ISBN: 978-1-5320-1751-3 (e)

Print information available on the last page.

iUniverse rev. date: 02/23/2017

This book is dedicated to

Drew DeBlasio

CONTENTS

ILLUSTRATIONS

The cover photo is the **Trenton Junction Train Station**, circa 1883 and is from the author's collection.

The photograph of the **Trenton Junction Hotel** is from the author's collection.

The photographs of **George Zinn and J.R. Mackie's air accident** are courtesy of Andy Heins, National Waco Club.

The **contract for brickwork** on the old Trenton Junction School, on Reading Hotel letterhead, is from the author's collection.

The Old Foundry at Trenton Junction is from the Hagley Museum & Library, "Wilbraham Brake & Blower Co at Trenton Junction," Warren-Ehret Co. Photo Albums, #2002251_039.

A colleague of mine once said to me, "You West Trenton people are very territorial!" It's true. We are. And with good reason. The roughly one square mile neighborhood of Trenton Junction—now larger and called West Trenton—is more than just a neighborhood in Ewing Township. It has its own culture and history that, while a part of the larger township, is also unique and all its own. While there are other equally old neighborhoods in Ewing—such as Wilburtha and Ewingville—no other neighborhood shares the unique history and development that Trenton Junction does. And thanks to the post office, we even have our own zip code. When asked by outsiders where we are from, those from the "square mile" usually answer "West Trenton" rather than "Ewing."

I quickly learned while researching this book that, while the residents of West Trenton share a unique history, and know that we share a unique history, no one really knows what that history is. "You're just snobs for no reason!" decries another colleague from another neighborhood in Ewing. After researching this book, I think we now have a reason.

It should be noted that the various stories told in this book are not set out chronologically. Also, I tried to combine footnotes, providing a single footnote at the end of a "story" rather than several throughout. It is important to read the footnotes for two reasons: One, because there may be additional information pertaining to the story being told and two, because it is sometimes interesting to see from where the story came. I relied almost solely on newspaper accounts for this book. Thanks to the phenomenal database, *Newspapers.com*, I was able to find (to my surprise) stories about Trenton Junction in newspapers from as far away as California!

This history of the Trenton Junction years is by no means exhaustive and complete. A frustrating problem with newspaper research is that the newspapers did not always follow a story through to its completion: There are stories where the reader is left hanging, wondering how the events played out. That is one of the difficulties with history—it is not necessarily "history" while it is happening, rather it is "current events." What may have been common knowledge a century ago is now often forgotten because nobody bothered to write it down.

The story of Trenton Junction is also a glimpse into rural Victorian era life in America. The advent of the steam railway, electric trolley, automobiles and the airplane all contributed to the growth and evolution of the hamlet of Birmingham into the town of Trenton Junction.

The history covered spans the 56 years from the advent of the railroad that led to the creation of the Junction in 1876 to 1932, when the town changed its name to West Trenton. A couple chapters of early history set the stage for the Trenton Junction Years and an appendix provides a glimpse into the makeup of the citizenry of Trenton Junction in 1930.

Mark W. Falzini
West Trenton, 2016

ACKNOWLEDGMENTS

There are many people to thank for their help with this book. First and foremost, I am indebted to my late Professors John Karras and Thomas Faughnan of Trenton State College (The College of New Jersey) History Department. They were my mentors during my time there as a history major and both played a major role in developing my passion for history, research, and writing.

I would like to thank my friends Wayne McDaniel, Margaret Sudhakar, and Dale Perry for their input and their much appreciated help editing my manuscript. Thank you to William H. Kale, Judith Engster Kale, Linda Kale, Barrie Kale, Kim Munley, Beth Larkin, JoAnne Tesauro, Tommy Sellaro, Michele DiRenza Levine, Jessica Bonds, Patty Garrison, Oliver Sissman, Gregg Senko and Lloyd Gardner for their encouragement when I decided to finally write a history of Trenton Junction. Also to Drew DeBlazio and Thomas Tighue who have provided lots of inspiration by sharing their passion for local history on Facebook.

Before their deaths in 2001, my father, Michael Falzini, and neighbor John "Jake" Garzio both sat with me and let me interview them about their lives growing up in Trenton Junction.

I am also grateful to Andy Heins of the National Waco Club who graciously provided photographs of George Zinn's plane wreck and Lynsey Sczechowicz, the Audiovisual Reference Archivist at the Hagley Museum and Library for providing the photograph of the old Winner Manufacturing building.

Like Mark Falzini, I am also a lifelong resident of today's West Trenton. Over the years, especially during other writing projects, Mark has always hinted that there was a "Trenton Junction" book coming. I am delighted that it has finally arrived and with more history and surprises than I ever imagined. *One Square Mile: A History of Trenton Junction, New Jersey* is a gem for current and former residents and anyone looking for a small town history at the turn of the century.

West Trenton is not really small town living as you might think of it—not Mayberry or Cabot Cove as those fictional towns happily depict. But there is something special about this place that has lasted for my lifetime and hopefully will continue into the future. I would like to think that most people are aware that the main intersection that we pass through each day is where General Washington divided his troops on the march to Trenton in 1776. I am also thankful that a marker exists memorializing this historic event. Mark, however, has now captured a period of history that brought transportation, and thereby the ability to enhance communication and industry, to a small, quiet farming community. This is the history that the general public may not be aware of—or, more likely, just takes for granted.

If you have always lived in West Trenton you will hear the trains and airplanes—but you will not *notice* them. They blend into the soundtrack of "home" and so you may give them little thought. In *One Square Mile,* Mark takes us to the beginning of Trenton Junction with the advent of the train community and all the events that surround becoming a town of rail travel—both freight and passenger. Later on, the addition of the airport brings another type of transportation to this small town. Trenton Junction becomes a destination.

More important, *One Square Mile* provides a glimpse into the lives of the people who have made this area their home. As I read back over 125 years ago, some of the names are still familiar as generations have stayed in this little town. It is magnificent to read about the patriotism, political disagreements, crime and passion that existed all those years ago. Issues were really not that different from today. Notably, Trenton Junction was a place for immigrants to settle and they were welcomed and blended into the town.

One of my former colleagues mentioned to me how lucky I was to have stayed in the "neighborhood" where I grew up. She was thinking in terms of having lifelong friends and acquaintances. While I am blessed to have those lifelong connections, it is also meaningful to know I have been part of a town that has played such a significant part in the development of the country and this area.

Mark Falzini has given us an opportunity to walk the roads of Trenton Junction as they transformed into the roads we walk today in West Trenton. *One Square Mile* is a well-researched, fascinating look at the history of Trenton Junction.

Dale K. Perry
December 12, 2016

Hoham
Taptaopamm
Mecoppe
Weheending
Lummassecon
Pleeze
Mehekizbhue
Caponoconickon
Nahusing
Mehkeekan
Shawonna

These eleven members of the Lenni Lenape—all *sachem*, or leaders of the tribe—were among the original citizens and nominal "land owners" of what was to become the hamlet of Birmingham and later the village of Trenton Junction. In the time before the land even had a name, the Lenape Indians roamed the area, establishing settlements along what was later called the Delaware River.

Europeans did not arrive until around 1675. Edward Byllynge was an English Governor of the Colony of West Jersey from 1680 to 1687. Through him, Quakers in England received deeds to land in West Jersey. On July 29, 1687, a forty-seven-year-old Englishman from Yorkshire named Thomas Hutchinson became one such Quaker landowner in what later was known as Ewing Township. Hutchinson's

Manor, as his property was called, consisted of 2,500 acres and covered 30 percent of modern Ewing Township.[1]

Thomas Hutchinson died intestate in 1689 and his sole heir was his son, John. Some seven years later, April 10, 1696 marked the beginning of the breakup of Thomas Hutchinson's original 2,500 acre manor tract. It was on this date that John Hutchinson conveyed 600 acres to John Bryerley.[2]

On November 15, 1699, Hutchinson deeded 650 acres to John Watson and Richard Eayre of Burlington County. On March 21, 1699, John Watson conveyed his ownership of that land over to Richard Eayre. Eayre now owned 810 acres along the Delaware River.[3] John Hutchinson conveyed another 400 acres out of Hutchinson's Manor to Andrew Heath on February 24, 1699.[4]

Although the early land purchases in the Ewing area were occurring in the late 17th century, European colonists did not inhabit the area until the beginning of the 18th century. The landowners, such as Thomas Hutchinson, usually lived in Burlington, Hopewell or other surrounding areas, provided they had actually immigrated to this side of the Atlantic. That said, it is believed that Hutchinson did eventually settle on his estate thereby becoming the first European settler in Ewing Township.[5]

The earliest European settlers in area came from Newtown, Long Island. Among those early settlers were Nathaniel Moore and his

---

[1] Falzini, Mark W. *Hutchinson's Manor*. Unpublished Manuscript. September 2006, page 1.

[2] ibid. Page 30-31.

[3] ibid. Page 31.

[4] ibid. Page 34.

[5] It should be noted that the area was not known at this time as Ewing Township. Originally, the area was part of Hopewell Township, which was in Burlington County. In 1713, Hopewell Township was removed from Burlington County and became part of the newly established Hunterdon County. From 1719, when the City of Trenton was founded, until 1834, the area was called Trenton Township. On February 22, 1834, the name was changed to Ewing Township in honor of Charles Ewing, the late Chief Justice of the New Jersey Supreme Court. It became part of Mercer County after its establishment in 1838.

wife, Joanna Prudden. They arrived in 1708 after Nathaniel bought "500 acres of land about 2 miles from Pennington on which he lived until his death on September 6, 1759...".[6] The property transferred to his son, Captain John Moore, and then, after his death in 1768, to Nathaniel's grandson, John C. Moore. He, in turn, died in 1815, leaving his property in what is now West Trenton to his children, John C., Elizabeth, Sarah and Charles.[7]

In 1816, John C. Moore, his brother Charles, his sister Elizabeth's husband the Rev. Asa Dunham, and his sister Sarah's husband George Hunt sold their father's property in West Trenton to Asa Fish for $3,920. The property they sold was "...part of a tract of land commonly known as *Hutchinson's Manor.*" It consisted of approximately 20 ¾ acres and was bounded on one side by "...the lane that leads to Green's new ferry" and also by the road that was "...near the (formerly) Union Tavern."[8]

On March 17, 1869, Asa Fish's heirs sold the property to Charles H. Walker, a local businessman, for $8,500. There was a house on the land that was not part of the sale. According to the deed, "...excepting and reserving thereout, a certain house and lot of land devised by Asa Fish, deceased, to his wife Rachel Ann Fish, said house and lot being opposite the dwelling house of Israel Fish [his brother] on the southwest corner of the crops road and being one hundred and twenty feet along the main road leading to the Yardleyville Delaware Bridge and sixty feet along the main road leading from [??] town to Trenton."[9]

When Charles Walker bought the Fish property, it came with certain stipulations attached to it. Walker,

---

[6] Stoupe, Ethel. "Origins of the Jersey Settlement of Rowan County, North Carolina." 1996. http://www.tamu.edu/ccbn/dewitt/mckstmerjersey.htm.

[7] Cooley, Eli F. and William S. Cooley. "Genealogy of Early Settlers in Trenton and Ewing 'Old Hunterdon County' New Jersey." 1883.

[8] Deed: John C. Moore, et al, to Asa Fish, 1816. Hunterdon County Deeds. Book 25 page 475.

[9] Deed: Asa I. Fish, et al, to Charles H. Walker. 1869. Mercer County Deeds. Book 74 page 347.

his heirs, executors, administrators or assigns, covenants that he shall never use said premises or cause the same to be used for the sale of cider, beer, or any intoxicating liquors whatever, or for any manufacturing purposes whatever, and that no slaughter house shall ever be erected thereon, and that no druggist or druggists shall sell or dispose o[f] any prescription from a regular practicing physician, whose certificate or diploma is duly filed according to law. And also that no livery or public stables or public laundry, or fish market shall ever be erected thereon nearer the line of said avenues than 20 feet. And also, that no privy-vault, cesspool or water closet shall ever be erected thereon, except it be built of brick and cement, the walls of which must be eight inches in thickness and must be laid up in and covered with cement, so as to be perfectly water-tight. And also that no house or cottage shall ever be erected on said Avenues that cost less than two thousand dollars."[10]

The property that Charles Walker purchased was near that of George Howell, another prominent Trenton Junction businessman. Their estates bordered Old River Road, a roadway that replaced an Indian trail that ran north and south, stretching from near Trenton north to Jacob's Creek. Today, this road is known as Sullivan Way, Grand Avenue and Bear Tavern Road. About five miles north of Trenton, Old River Road intersected with "...the lane that leads to Green's new ferry," today's West Upper Ferry Road. This intersection played an important part in early American history.

---

[10]   Warranty Deed. March 12, 1903. Mercer County Deeds. Book 578 pages 58-60.

CHAPTER 1

THE BIRMINGHAM CROSSROAD

THE HAMLET OF BIRMINGHAM, named for the town of Birmingham, England, cropped up around the intersection of an ancient Indian trail called the Old River Road and the crossroad that led from Scotch Road to the Delaware River, today called West Upper Ferry Road. There was a tavern near here, formerly known as The Union Tavern. It was a quiet and nondescript hamlet, where nothing much ever happened. That is until one cold, snowy morning in 1776.

The American War for Independence had been raging for several months with nothing but defeat after defeat for the American armies. George Washington needed to change that. His troops' enlistments were soon to be up and he would have no choice but to allow his discouraged soldiers the opportunity to decline re-enlistment. Washington needed a victory.

General Washington and his troops were encamped in Valley Forge, Pennsylvania. Unbeknownst to the British, he moved his troops to the shores of the Delaware, near Maconkey's Ferry. In the dark hours shortly after midnight on Christmas night, Washington and his troops crossed the Delaware into New Jersey. His plan was to march on to Trenton, and surprise the Hessian mercenaries who were holed-up in the barracks there, hung-over and exhausted from their Christmas celebrations.

General Washington marched his men across Jacob's Creek and down the Old River Road towards Trenton. The road was snow covered and the air bitter and frigid. They approached the hamlet of Birmingham and when they reached the crossroad the next phase of Washington's plan was invoked. At the intersection of modern day Bear Tavern Road/Grand Avenue and West Upper Ferry Road, Washington divided his troops. "One column under the command of General Nathanael Greene, approached the city from the northwest… The other column, led by General John Sullivan, marched down the Old River Road (Grand Avenue—Sullivan Way) and entered Trenton from the southwest. This brilliant strategy resulted in a major military victory and became the turning point of the American Revolutionary War."[11]

———

Today there are approximately 20 separate roads in West Trenton proper. Originally there were three. The three major public roadways date back to the 18th century and have been known by various names over the years.

Scotch Road, which used to incorporate both current day Scotch Road and Parkway Avenue, was surveyed and established as a public road in 1741. It led from Trenton by way of the Pennington Road into the heart of Birmingham. Here it merged with the "road that led to Green's new ferry"—the upper ferry road—and it ran down to Greensboro, modern day Wilburtha. During the late nineteenth and early twentieth centuries, the upper ferry road was known as Ewing Avenue.

Modern day Lower Ferry Road had its start in 1768 and was known as the Old Ferry Road and ran from the river to the Old River Road.

Old River Road—the former Indian trail—was surveyed sometime before 1766. The stretch through the heart of Birmingham—from today's

---

[11] From the inscription on the historical marker located at the intersection of Bear Tavern Road and West Upper Ferry Road in West Trenton, New Jersey.

train crossing to the "crossroads"—became known as Grand Avenue and was prime real estate for the country homes of the wealthy residents of the surrounding area. "By the turn of the century, Grand Avenue had become the most prestigious address in Ewing Township." The stretch of the road north of the crossroads was eventually named after the Bear Tavern. The lower section below the "Old Ferry Road" was officially called the *Ewing and Trenton Turnpike* but locally it became known as The Asylum Road—it passed between the State Psychiatric Hospital "asylum" and "Oaklands," the Woodruff estate that, in 1897, became the Trenton Country Club. Eventually, the Asylum Road and the section of Grand Avenue below the train crossing became known as Sullivan Way.[12]

The 1890s saw proposals for new public roads in Trenton Junction. In April 1894, for example, a proposal was made to open a new road leading from Trenton Junction to the Scotch Road "which will pass through the DeCou farm, which will be laid out in building lots. This new road will take considerable travel from the old Birmingham Road and make a route that is three-quarters of a mile shorter between the Junction and Trenton."[13]

The following year, there was a movement calling for a new road from Stuyvesant Avenue to Trenton Junction: "If this road is open it will take a great deal of travel from the Ewing and Trenton Turnpike. Many complaints have been made of late against the Turnpike Company for not maintaining a good road. Several farmers who use the road have refused to pay toll on account of the bad condition of the road…it is said that application will soon be made to the court to have the road opened here to the public."[14]

In April 1896, however, the push for the new roadway hit a roadblock. It was requested that a commission be appointed to investigate the necessity of the road. The road was to pass "…through the lands of C.H. Walker, G.L. Howell, George Pierson, Charles Scudder, and J.

---

[12] Hand, Susan C. "Mercer County Historic Sites Survey: Ewing, East Windsor, West Windsor and Washington Townships." Kings & Hand, Princeton: September 2, 1988.

[13] Trenton Times, April 23, 1894.

[14] Trenton Evening Times, September 12, 1895.

Foreman Rose. The road [was] to run from the Junction to a point in the Lower Ferry Road." Charles Walker opposed the opening of the road "...because it would be useless and of great expense." As it was, the road required two bridges which alone would cost $5,000.

According to the law, ten Freeholders had to petition for the road, which was done, except that, as in most things involving politicians, there was a bit of a scandal. It turns out that one of the petitioners, J. Lincoln Knight, was not actually a Freeholder, "...as his only real estate is a cemetery lot which the law does not construe as real estate ownership, because it is held under restrictions not common to real estate."[15] The project, it appears, never came to fruition.

The aforementioned Ewing-Trenton Turnpike (aka the Asylum Road) was at one time a toll road. However, by March 1896, the Ewing Turnpike had been "thrown open to the public without tolls." This resulted in travel on the road increasing "considerably" and "...very many farmers now use the road who formerly traveled by way of the Scotch Road."[16] It was the leading roadway to the Asylum, Wilburtha and Trenton Junction. "It is traveled extensively each day by many milkmen from the farms in Ewing Township, and is one of the favorite roads of drivers and cyclists."[17]

By the following year, the Trenton and Ewing Turnpike Commission had ceased to exist, and "little to nothing" had been done to maintain the Asylum Road. "It is rough in some places and covered with loose stones. An effort is being made to have it macadamized by the freeholders."[18]

In October 1897, a resolution was passed by the Freeholders to have the Asylum Road paved. They also "...decided to build a new bridge over Gold Run in front of Charles Scudder's place."[19] In 1899, bids were

---

[15] Trenton Evening Times, April 10, 1896.

[16] Trenton Evening Times, March 19, 1896.

[17] Trenton Evening Times, June 14, 1899.

[18] Trenton Evening Times. September 11, 1897.

[19] Trenton Evening Times, October 27, 1897. Gold Run is the stream that runs through the New Jersey Manufactures Insurance Company's property which was originally Charles Scudder's farm. The bridge was built where modern Sullivan Way crosses the stream.

received by the Board of Chosen Freeholders for the macadamizing project. Contracts were awarded to Robert A. Montgomery for macadamizing both the Asylum and (West) Upper Ferry Roads. He had bid $10,475 for the Asylum Road and $3,425 for West Upper Ferry Road.[20]

By mid-June, 1899, work had begun on the roads. The macadamizing project for the Asylum Road began "…at Parkside Avenue, Cadwalader Place and extended to Birmingham…a distance of about three miles." The upper Ferry Road project began "…at Birmingham and extended to the Delaware and Raritan Canal…a distance of about one mile."[21]

Strangely, the stretch of Grand Avenue, between the Asylum Road and (West) Upper Ferry Road—the two roads macadamized in 1899—was not itself paved for another twenty years! Bids for the construction of curbs, gutters and sidewalks along Grand Avenue were accepted in 1919. In April 1920, the Board of Chosen Freeholders approved the plans for paving Grand Avenue with cement and concrete "from the railway tunnel to the Upper Ferry Road." The cost was estimated between $45,000 and $50,000 and the Trenton & Mercer County Traction Corporation, which ran the trolley along the road into town, bore a portion of the cost.[22]

---

[20] Trenton Evening Times, April 6, 1899.

[21] Trenton Evening Times, April 5, 1899.

[22] Trenton Evening Times, September 4, 1919; April 7, 1920; April 27, 1920; April 28, 1920. The final cost was $54,325.45. That was the lowest bid, proposed by Antonio DiLucia. The only other bidder for the project was the Hill Construction Company with a proposal of $68,380.97. Another sign of the struggle for modernization was the difficulty in street lighting. In 1901, Trenton Junction was in need of a lamplighter. There were street lamps all around the town, "but the township appropriation being so small no one will bother with them." Thomas Doman was trying at that time to get the contract to install gas lamps. It was not until February 1913 that the Ewing Township Committee met to discuss "Committeeman W.T. Connard's proposition to install electric lights in Trenton Junction streets." (Trenton Times, September 13, 1901; Trenton Evening Times, February 28, 1913.)

CHAPTER 2

MAKING OF A JUNCTION

Aᴀ ꜰᴛᴇʀ ᴛʜᴇ ᴇxᴄɪᴛᴇᴍᴇɴᴛ ᴏꜰ Washington's army passing through, Birmingham returned to being a quiet, unassuming rural hamlet of dirt roads and farms. Then, the trains came.

Railroad transportation was first developed in the early nineteenth century by George Stephenson in England. Railroads in England were able to drop the cost of shipping by 60–70 percent[23], a fact not lost on American businessmen. Transportation by rail became vital to the success of the industrial revolution as well as to the settlement of the West.

The first chartered railroad in the United States—the Baltimore and Ohio—broke ground on July 4, 1828, when "…the first spadeful of earth was turned over by the last surviving signer of the Declaration of Independence, 91-year-old Charles Carroll."[24] By the 1870s, railroad construction increased dramatically. Between 1871 and 1900, over 170,000 miles of track had been laid.

On May 12, 1874, the Delaware and Bound Brook Railroad was incorporated in New Jersey and track construction began on October 7th. On May 1, 1876, this company began operation on a track system

---

[23] www.ushistory.org/us/25b.asp.

[24] ibid.

that stretched from the Delaware River, where it connected to the North Pennsylvania Railroad in Yardley, Pennsylvania, to Bound Brook, New Jersey. There it connected with the Central Railroad of New Jersey. It included a short branch line from Trenton Junction to the Warren Street Station in Trenton.

Meanwhile, in Pennsylvania, the Philadelphia and Reading Railway Company was expanding. Founded on April 4, 1833, this line ran between Philadelphia and Reading, Pennsylvania. It was one of the nation's first railroads and became one of the most prosperous companies in the country. It was originally founded as a freight line, to haul anthracite coal from mines in northeastern Pennsylvania to Philadelphia.

On May 14, 1879, the Philadelphia and Reading "leased the Northern Pennsylvania Railroad, including the Delaware and Bound Brook" and later renamed itself *The Reading Company*. Included in the leasing of the Delaware and Bound Brook was "...a branch railroad known as 'The Trenton Branch' that extended from its connection with the main line of the Delaware and Bound Brook Railroad at a point known as Lathrop or Trenton Junction, in the county of Mercer..."[25] The Reading Railroad, as it was commonly called, shared its tracks with the Baltimore & Ohio, which provided freight and passenger service most notably for its famous *Royal Blue Line*.

In 1881, a station was built just off the Old River Road about a mile south of Birmingham "at the intersection of the main track of the railroad and a spur line to downtown Trenton."[26] Designed by Philadelphia architect Frank Furness, whose style was noted for its "eclectic, muscular, [and] often idiosyncratically scaled buildings," it featured a large clock tower on one end and was located directly across from Carrigg Avenue, where the rail line split and headed into

---

[25] Report of the Operations of the Philadelphia and Reading Railroad Company and Reading Coal and Iron Company. 1877.

[26] Ewing Township Historic Preservation Society. "History of Ewing Township." http://ethps.org/history/history.htm.

Trenton.[27] The following year, Birmingham was officially renamed *Trenton Junction* "...when a post office was established" and Trenton Junction became Ewing Township's first subdivision.[28]

In May 1929, the Reading Railroad Company announced that the station designed by Furness was to be replaced. The new station, according to the official announcement, was to be located several yards down the tracks from the old station, "just east of Asylum Road, where it will be easily accessible by automobile...Private drives on both sides of the railroad will lead to the station grounds, which are to be large, allowing parking of cars by those using the trains." Stairways, on each side of the railroad bridge, made it possible for pedestrians to easily reach the train platforms as well. According to the railroad, two concrete covered train platforms—eastbound and westbound—would be installed, "each 600 feet long, starting at the bridge over Asylum Road and extending eastward." The new station was renamed the *West*

---

[27] Between 1878 and 1906, Frank Furness had designed nearly 200 buildings for the Reading, the B&O, and the Pennsylvania Railroads. Eventually, his bold style fell out of fashion and many of his significant works were demolished in the early 20th century, including the station at Trenton Junction. (wikipedia/wiki/Frank Furness). See also www.frankfurness.org. Newspaper accounts, however, mention that Captain Biand de Morainville, a Philadelphia architect and formerly an engineer in the French army, had completed the architectural designs for the new station at Trenton Junction. While this is probably true, it was indeed Frank Furness who had the final design. "As a salaried employee of the Philadelphia and Reading Railroad between 1880 and 1885, Furness created a de facto corporate image by applying his unique design and sensibility to railroad stations...throughout eastern Pennsylvania and northern New Jersey." (Preston Thayer, "The Railroad Designs of Frank Furness: Architecture and Corporate Imagery in the Late Nineteenth Century" (http://repository.upenn.edu/dissertationsAAI9321487/).

[28] Tesauro, Joann. *Ewing Township*. Arcadia Books, North Carolina. 2002. It should be noted that there was a small station already located in Trenton Junction and that the railroads referred to it as Trenton Junction as early as 1873. A time schedule printed in the October 11, 1876 *Brooklyn Daily Eagle* stated that "all trains [on the Bound Brook Route] connect at Trenton Junction to and from Trenton."

Trenton Station and in June 1932, the post office and town followed suit.[29]

As railroads expanded, so did the workforce. While the Transcontinental Railroad at the time employed mostly Chinese immigrants, the Reading hired Italians—mostly from the Abruzzo region in central Italy. By the turn of the century, one hundred and sixty Italian immigrants were employed on the Reading Railroad.[30]

In January 1906, the Italian workforce demanded an increase of 1½¢ per hour in their pay. Up to this point, they were receiving 13½¢ per hour for working a 10-hour day. The company, naturally, refused the pay increase. The Italians went on strike.

Initially there was no violence, however the strike leaders placed six men around the Trenton Junction Train Station "...armed with stilettos and pick handles to prevent any possible desertion from the ranks." A number of the workers were willing to return to the job however they feared for their lives and so the strike continued.

The next day the strikers were told that unless they returned to work at their old wages, the railroad would evict them from their company-owned housing and fired. The peaceful strike turned violent. On January 10, 1906, more than 100 strikers and six Reading Railway detectives "had a hand-to-hand battle...The Italians swarmed about the passenger station in a threatening manner and Detective Rowland Mitchell ordered them back. They refused to comply and the detective and his assistants drove them from the place. This angered the Italians and they made a rush for the detectives. A hand-to-hand scuffle followed and then the detectives pulled their revolvers and threatened to shoot. The sight of the weapons halted the Italians, although several...pulled stilettos and declared they would use them if the detectives did not put up their pistols."[31]

Shortly before one o'clock that afternoon, Detective Mitchell captured the ringleader of the strikers and held him in the waiting

---

[29] Philadelphia Inquirer, May 12, 1929.

[30] Trenton Times, January 9, 1906.

[31] Trenton Times, January 10, 1906.

room of the railroad station. "The Italians left the woods and crowded around the station and demanded the release of their leader. They were told that he would be sent to prison."

The strikers "held a short conference" and finally agreed to return to work without any concessions, provided the railroad guaranteed their leader's freedom. "This the railroaders conceded and the entire gang went to work."[32]

The housing that the Railroad had provided for the immigrant workers was located across the tracks from the train station. There, the Reading Railroad built a makeshift "shanty village." Locally known as "the railroad camp," it consisted of 19 buildings and by 1916 over 300 Italians were living there, making Trenton Junction the "first ethnic enclave in Ewing Township."[33]

The buildings were set in an L-shape. One wing of buildings was reserved for railroad workers and their families. The other was set aside for transient workers who would come to work on the railroad for a short time, for just a few days or weeks, before moving on to other work.

There were four units to a building, two upstairs and two downstairs, with one entrance. The family housing had double out-houses that were shared, two families to a side. "Every so often they would have a clean-up job—they called those people *Honey Dippers.*" The housing for the transient laborers was a little more upscale. They had access to a mess hall, hot and cold running water, showers, and they had flush toilets in their outhouses that emptied into a cistern.[34]

The buildings were constructed of plain brick walls, about four inches thick, with a plaster wall on the inside, and the flat roof was made of tin. There were no storm windows, so ice would form, sometimes up to two inches thick. The rooms were heated by a wood burning stove that could also burn coal. "They would burn wood

---

[32]   Trenton Times, January 10, 1906.

[33]   Hand, Susanne C. "Mercer County Historic Sites Survey: Ewing, East Windsor, West Windsor and Washington Townships." Kings & Hand, Princeton: September 2, 1988, page 8.

[34]   Garzio, John "Jake". *Interview with the author.* May 12, 1991.

during the day and coal at night, because it burned slower." The coal came from coal cars that the Reading Railroad would bring to the stations along the line. It would stay at the station just long enough for the workers to gather enough coal to last a week or two before moving on to the next station.

> Wood for the stoves came from two sources—old railroad ties or oak trees from nearby woods. "They would cut the oak into four-foot lengths with crosscut saws and then haul them out of the woods. They used two-wheeled carts with a pair of shafts in the front. One guy would put the shafts under his arms and pull while two or three others would push from the back. Once back at camp, they would have wood cutting parties on the weekends. They would cut the wood by hand, but later, once cars were available, they would jack up a car and put a belt around one of the wheels that would turn a circular saw. They would saw like crazy! When they finished, they would then split the wood and stack it for the winter."[35]

There was never a shortage of food in the railroad camp. Everyone had a garden and they raised goats, chickens, rabbits and even sheep. "Some goats were strictly milk fed and raised to be eaten. The goat's milk was used for drinking instead of cow's milk." They also canned their food for the winter. "They canned everything in sight!" Orders could be placed for groceries and supplies not available locally and they would be delivered once a week.

The railroad camp also had its own commissary, where the laborers could buy cigarettes and tobacco, and canned goods. "They would buy $2.00 packs of tickets, and each ticket was worth 5¢, 10¢, 20¢ and so on. To pay for something, you handed the clerk your ticket book and he would punch the required tickets. Sometimes he would cheat you. Instead of punching 30¢ for something, he might punch 35¢. If you went in there drunk he might punch your whole ticket book!"

---

[35] Garzio, John "Jake". *Interview with the author.* May 12, 1991.

Come payday, the laborers would "have a ball." There was very little gambling, but they would drink. "They would drink anything under the sun! And they had bootleggers down there that would make wine." Barrels of wine were produced and sold to anyone in town who wanted to buy it. Bocce and card games would be played on the weekend, not for money but for bottles of wine. The railroad camp was a fun place to be. "There was always something going on down there, we kids loved it."[36]

The railroad camp was finally abandoned shortly after the Second World War and was eventually torn down during the 1950s.

---

[36] Falzini, Michael J. *Interview with the author.* May 12, 1991 and John "Jake" Garzio, *Interview with the author.* May 12, 1991.

CHAPTER 3

GETTING SOME TRACTION

THE TRAINS WERE NOT alone in transforming the quiet hamlet of Birmingham into the bustling suburban village of Trenton Junction. They had the help of...*trolleys!*

Traction vehicles, also known as street cars, trams, and trolleys, "were the backbone of local transportation throughout the United States until they were displaced by automobiles and busses after World War II." [37] They ran along city streets on tracks similar to train tracks.

Originally, trolleys were pulled by animals; however the 1880s saw the arrival of electric trolleys. "Each vehicle was independently powered by electric motors and..." they received their electric power from an overhead wire by way of a wheel attached to a pole called a *trolley pole.* "The rapid growth of streetcar systems led to the widespread ability of people to live outside of a city and commute into it for work on a daily basis...streetcars operated between cities and served remote,

---

[37] Piedmont and Western Railroad Club. http://www.pwrr.org/traction/trolley. html.

even rural areas."[38] The spread of trolley lines encouraged Ewing's—and Birmingham's—suburbanization.[39]

It was not until after 1900 that two electric trolley lines were built in Ewing Township:

> One trolley line, which crossed the eastern end of the township, was built from Trenton to Princeton about 1902 by the *Trenton, Lawrenceville, and Princeton Trolley Company*, and was later absorbed into the *Trenton & Mercer County Traction Company*…The other line, the more important one for Ewing, operated on Pennington Road from Trenton to Hopewell. It was completed before 1905 by the *Mercer County Traction Company*, and it served a much larger portion of the township.[40]

While the general public of Trenton Junction wanted the trolley, there were some issues that had to be overcome first. On May 3, 1903, the Delaware Valley Traction Company requested a franchise from Ewing Township. There were objections, but the company had secured the consent of 51% of the property owners along the proposed route. On June 27th, a special meeting of the Ewing Township Committee was held so that they could meet with the promotors of the Traction Company in hopes of ironing out any lingering issues. Unfortunately, final action was not taken "…and the original intent of the meeting was lost in a flow of objections from property owners [north of] Trenton Junction who have opposed the road because there is a desire on the part of the company to use parts of a public highway, about 2,500 feet between Trenton and Titusville, and also because of the prospect of slight disturbance by trolley noises, of the quiet summer homes."

---

[38] https://en.wikipedia.org/wiki/Streetcars_in_North_America.

[39] Hand, Susanne C. "Mercer County Historic Sites Survey: Ewing, East Windsor, West Windsor and Washington Townships." Kings & Hand, Princeton: September 2, 1988. Page 8.

[40] Hand, Susanne C. "Mercer County Historic Sites Survey: Ewing, East Windsor, West Windsor and Washington Townships." Kings & Hand, Princeton: September 2, 1988. Page 9.

Objections were so fierce that the trolley company decided to submit a new map. The new map defined the trolley routes "…either over a private right of way from Birmingham to [the] Hopewell Township line or that the line will follow the straight road from Birmingham over or alongside the Harbourton road instead of turning [left at] the upper ferry road and going to the river." [41]

Once the trolley line was established, it provided less expensive travel from Trenton to Trenton Junction than by train. However, the trolley took much longer to get there. In 1917, the journey from State and Broad Streets to the Trenton Country Club—across the street from the "asylum"—took 25 minutes and from the Country Club into Trenton Junction proper, another 7 to 11 minutes.

[41] Trenton Times, June 29, 1903.

CHAPTER 4

PARKS AND RECREATION

THERE ONCE WAS A time when Trenton Junction had a park. Named in honor of the 16th President, Lincoln Park had its grand opening on Thursday, May 17, 1883. The grand opening celebrations included shooting matches, dancing "…and amusements of all kinds." It was to be a "Day of pleasure for all." The park was located across from the train station and the railroad provided special trains from the corner of Warren and Tucker Streets in Trenton every thirty minutes, a return ticket costing just 10¢.

While picnics were popular in the park, the first major event held there was the Grand Field Encampment of Aaron Wilkes Post, No. 23, of the Grand Army of the Republic. This auspicious event was a week-long encampment of Civil War veterans. From Saturday, July 28 until Sunday August 5, 1883, there were to be "great attractions"—picnics, dancing, a concert by Winkler's Band, fireworks, sham fights and more![42] On Sundays there were camp meetings and religious services, with sacred music provided by Winkler's Band and singing by church choirs. Admission to the encampment, including round trip train fare from Trenton was 25¢ for adults and just 13¢ for children under twelve. Admission for locals who did not need to take the train was 15¢. On the first day of the encampment, trains ran every half hour from the Warren Street Station to Trenton Junction. The veterans paraded from their Post Headquarters on South Greene Street to Warren Street to board the trains.

By 1890, Lincoln Park had acquired a bad reputation, probably because its proximity to the train station made it an attractive hangout for tramps and hobos. On October 20th of that year, Charles H. Walker applied for a liquor license to sell beer and malt liquors "in less quantities than a quart" at the park. Because of the park's "bad reputation," the license was refused. However, the park remained in operation for a few more years. [43]

Another popular event that was usually held in Lincoln Park was the annual Harvest Home. A Harvest Home is a festival held in late August or early September, marking the end of the harvest period. It is an old English custom dating back to pagan times and is sometimes

---

[42] Professor Albert Winkler came from a family of German musicians who, for at least three generations, "occupied a prominent place in musical circles." He was the leader of the Seventh and Second Regiment Bands of the New Jersey National Guard and he conducted countless concerts and dances around the Trenton area. At one time he had one hundred musicians under his command, "each being a soloist on his respective instrument." The Winkler Brass Band "won high praise at Washington, DC, and other cities where they figured in important parades." (www.trentonhistory.org/His/Foreign.html; Trenton Evening Times, January 20, 1896 & July 12, 1921).

[43] Trenton Evening Times, May 16, 1883 & July 19, 1883; Trenton Times, July 20 & 27, 1883; Trenton Times, September 6, 1884; Trenton Times, August 31, 1887; Trenton Evening Times, June 7 1899. The Trenton Junction School held commencement exercises in the park in June 1894. The last mention of Lincoln Park that can be found in newspapers is in the June 7, 1899 edition of the Trenton Evening Times where it was announced that "The comrades of Aaron Wilkes Post No. 33" held another encampment in Trenton Junction. While not mentioned specifically, it can be assumed that the encampment was held at the park.

called a "harvest festival" or an "Ingathering" and is akin to today's Thanksgiving holiday.

Still popular in rural areas today, a harvest home usually features an overabundance of homemade food and desserts, and is especially known for "eating, merriment, contests [and] music." Oftentimes speeches are given by local politicians.[44]

The Harvest Home events held in Trenton Junction were quite popular, attracting many visitors from the surrounding area. Special trolleys and additional trains (with lowered fares!) connected Trenton to Trenton Junction. A round trip ride from Trenton cost just 25¢ in 1895.

Most often, the Harvest Home festivals were given by a local church group. An early Harvest Home advertised for in the *Trenton Times* in 1891 and 1892, announced that a Harvest Home would be given by the Ladies of Trinity M.E. Church. In 1895 the Ladies of the Ewing Presbyterian Church hosted. The Trenton Junction Improvement Society and their Ladies' Aid Society arranged for a harvest home for August 1907[45]. The event that year was to be held on the grounds of the Grange Hall to "help clear the Grange Hall of debt."[46]

In 1909, the Harvest Home was held on a Wednesday—August 18th. This year, in addition to the trolley and railroad, auto rides to and from the picnic grounds were being offered from E.M. Watson's toy store at 8 North Broad Street in Trenton. This exciting ride made the event a little bit more expensive. An auto ride to the picnic grounds, including

---

[44] www.wikipedia.org/wiki/Harvest_festival.

[45] The Trenton Junction Improvement Society was established on June 1, 1906 "by some of the most prominent men of Trenton Junction." Its principal objects and purposes were to promote social and moral life and to "generally improve conditions" in and around Trenton Junction. The chairman was Lester R. Weller and former Freeholder Benjamin Baldwin was the secretary of the meeting. The permanent officers elected that night were President Wilber Fisk, Vice President Lester Weller, Secretary Dr. E.B. Allen and Treasurer Benjamin Baldwin. (Trenton Times, June 2, 1906).

[46] Trenton Evening Times, July 13, 1907, August 26, 1907 and August 29, 1907. Grange Hall was another popular gathering place in Trenton Junction. Its precise location is unknown today.

supper, cost 75¢ (children 55¢), whereas if you took the trolley or train, tickets including supper were 50¢ (30¢ for children).[47]

The 1909 Harvest Home was to be a momentous event. Not only were there to be auto rides to and from Lincoln Park, Governor John F. Fort had agreed to attend. The Harvest Home was to be the first and only "entertainment of the kind in the State to boast the distinction of a visit from New Jersey's Chief Executive." This was the first time since 1891, when Governor Leon Abbett attended, that a sitting Governor addressed the crowd. In addition to the Governor, the Trenton Junction Improvement Association was able to secure Frank Berry, the State Treasurer of Pennsylvania, as a speaker.[48]

Politicians were popular speakers at the Harvest Home festivals. In 1907, Judge William M. Lanning spoke about "our constitutional liberties, how we acquired them and how they can be preserved" and Assemblyman Barber spoke about "the benefits which could be derived from such organizations as the Improvement Society" that hosted the event.[49]

Because the festivals were held relatively close to Election Day, many candidates for office would make an appearance. The 1908 Harvest Home featured Philip Freudenmacher, Thomas E. Raub, William L. Steward and Jedidiah G. Coleman, "candidates for Sheriff, all of whom made themselves known to every person in the assemblage."[50]

[47] Trenton Evening Times, August 17, 1909.

[48] Trenton Evening Times, July 7, 1909.

[49] The original article in the August 29, 1907 edition of the Trenton Evening Times stated his address was about "our constitutional *libraries*..." It is assumed that "liberties" was actually meant. William M. Lanning was a Ewing Township native. Born in 1849 in Ewingville, he was a local public school teacher. He had studied law and was elected city solicitor for Trenton in 1884. Then, three years later, he was appointed judge of the city district court. In 1903, he was elected to Congress, but resigned in 1904 when was appointed a judge in the US District Court for the District of New Jersey by President Theodore Roosevelt. In 1909, President Taft appointed him to the US Court of Appeals for the Third Circuit. Lanning School in Ewing Township was named in his honor.

[50] Trenton Evening Times, August 13, 1908.

Baseball has run through the veins of the residents of Trenton Junction since the 1890s, to the exclusion of other sports. The game's heyday was during the Great Depression of the 1930s, when the local team of under 20-year-olds played in the WPA sponsored league that was just one notch below semi-professional. Before there was a roster of local players, however, the Trenton Junction baseball team consisted of employees of the Philadelphia and Reading Railroad.

One of the earliest local games recorded in the press was "a remarkable game…the most notable game ever witnessed in this section" and it took place on June 23, 1896, on the grounds at Trenton Junction. One team was composed of clerks employed by the Reading Railroad and the other was made up of trainmen. "Over 2,000 spectators participated in the excitement occasioned by the desperate struggle, the nines being so evenly matched that the chances of victory alternated with provoking impartiality."[51]

The game ran into the sixteenth inning and was finally called on account of darkness. The score stood at 13 to 13. The paper reported that brilliant plays were frequent and the Trainmen's shortstop was injured by a "hot liner from John Malley's bat."

Games continued to be played each year against other local teams. During the last year of the nineteenth century and the early years of the 20th, teams such as the Hobsons of Trenton, the Trenton Field Club, WP Harringans, Globe Rubber, Willetts Pottery and the All-Cuban Baseball Team of Pennington Seminary went up against the Trenton Junction nine.

It was not until the spring of 1910 that a team made up of local residents was formed. On the evening of April 23rd, "the boys of Trenton Junction" held a meeting in the home of Benjamin Stokes —the fifteen-year-old son of Rudolf and Elizabeth Stokes—to organize a baseball team. They decided to make their new grounds by the school house. Ben Stokes was elected team manager and Hart Hill, president. Henry

---

[51] The Times (Philadelphia, Pennsylvania), The Evening Times (Washington, D.C.), June 23, 1896.

Jones was appointed groundskeeper. Their first game was played April 25, 1910, against the team from Wilburtha.[52]

The first ball field was on land owned by John Kurtz, across the street from the current location of Freddy's Tavern. The field was on the block bordered by Trenton Avenue, Railroad Avenue, and New Street. Right field was by Trenton Avenue. The second field was on Summit Avenue and was a "big open field."

The third field was located directly behind the current West Trenton Train Station. "It was a big open field and it had a billboard sign that [once] said 'VISIT ATLANTIC CITY.' John Rattico sometimes hit the billboard. He didn't hit the ball often, but when he did, he hit it hard. I remember one time he went right over it!"[53]

The Trenton Junction team would continue in one form or another for at least another 30 years, with each successive generation adding to its roster. "Eventually the team evolved in to a new team—the West Trenton team. This was formed with the help of Mr. John Ross who got us started. He took us to all the ball games in his dump truck—it was the only way to get to the game!"[54]

In 1940, under the sponsorship of local politician, philanthropist and baseball enthusiast, Steward "Stu" O'Donnell, the West Trenton O'Donnells, as they were known for that year, won the league championship.

"We had the best baseball team!"[55]

---

[52] Trenton Evening Times, April 25, 1910. Remarkably, the newspaper did not report on the team's first game! The first game to make it into the newspaper was played on May 1, 1910. The Trenton Junction baseball team defeated the Hopewell Crescents in an away game. "The game was a pitchers' battle from beginning to end, the final score being 4 to 3." (Trenton Evening Times, May 2, 1910).

[53] Hendrckson, Samuel. *Interview with the author.* July 26, 2007.

[54] Falzini, Michael J. *Interview with the author.* May 12, 1991.

[55] Garzio, John "Jake." *Interview with the author.* May 12, 1991. The author's father, Mike Falzini, and longtime Ewing Township Clerk Jake Garzio both played with the team during the 1930s.

CHAPTER 5

WHERE THE TRAINS ARE, HOTELS SOON FOLLOW

WITH THE POPULARITY OF rail travel, hotels inevitably appeared near rail stations, even in the smallest of towns. While there may not have been much to bring outsiders to Trenton Junction for extended visits, small town hotels served other useful purposes.

Small town hotels did not cater only to rail passengers and travelling salesmen. They were also frequented by the local residents. Hotels gave locals "…a place to come for organized social events, be they on a weekly, monthly, seasonal, or other cycle," or one of a kind special events. "They had a place to host family affairs. Hotels provided spaces to just plain relax in, places to meet friends merely to socialize…Hotels also represented impressive venues where out-of-town dignitaries, for example, might be welcomed and entertained."[56]

Trenton Junction was no exception and, in March 1892, John Armstrong purchased a 200 foot by 225 foot plot from the

---

[56] Jakle, John A. and Keith A. Sculle. "America's Main Street Hotels: Transiency and Community in the Early Auto Age." University of Tennessee Press, 2009. Page 46.

Pennsylvania and Reading Railroad for $500 with the intent of building a hotel. He sold the property to Jacob Kurtz and, it was announced on January 31, 1893, that he was going to build a two-story brick hotel for $10,000. Construction began straight away and by November 8th the Trenton Junction Hotel opened directly across from the station.[57]

The hotel proved so popular that on May 16, 1894, it was announced that "an addition will be built to the new hotel at Trenton Junction, extending from the south wing parallel with the east end of the building. It will consist in the second story of a number of large bedrooms, while the lower floor will be laid out in a large and handsome billiard room. The work will be started next week under the direction of Contractor Israel Loutz. William Guy, of Yardley [Pennsylvania], has secured the contract for the plastering and mason work."[58] The contract for tin roofing, galvanizing and the furnishing of the hardware for the alterations was held by Howard Harrold of Trenton Junction and Comly & Aaron furnished the lumber.[59]

The hotel did, indeed, serve as a gathering spot for locals for various occasions. There was, naturally, a saloon in the hotel which was assuredly frequented by the locals. In October 1896, Kurtz renewed his liquor license for $100.[60] On March 1, 1898, Charles Edinger won a bicycle at a drawing held at Kurtz's hotel.

In 1901, Kurtz was advertising in the *Trenton Times* suggesting that "for an outing, pleasant drive and [a] little recreation," motorists should stop at the Trenton Junction Hotel "for refreshments." He also made it known in the advertisement that there was a "Bell phone" available and that the roads were Macadamized, ostensibly providing for a smoother ride![61]

Both the Ewing Township Committee and the Mercer County

---

[57] Trenton Times, January 31, 1893; March 28, 1893; and November 8, 1893.

[58] Trenton Times, May 16, 1894.

[59] Trenton Times, May 19, 1894.

[60] Trenton Evening Times, October 28, 1896.

[61] Trenton Times, July 24, 1901.

Board of Chosen Freeholders would occasionally hold meetings at the hotel. In August 1906, after an inspection tour of various new roads that were in the course of construction in the township, the "Road Committee of the Board of Freeholders" was "entertained at luncheon at Kurtz's Hotel" by Freeholder Franklin Burroughs.[62]

Picture, if you can, the small towns featured in old movies and television shows, where nearly the entire population of young and old alike gathered for parades and rallies. This really did happen, and it happened at the Trenton Junction Hotel. On October 21, 1904, the Ewing Republicans were planning to hold a mass meeting at the hotel, preceded by a "big parade, which will consist of the Ewing Township Republican Club and the City Invincibles of Trenton."[63] The parade was to be headed by Winkler's Band. The parade was to start at the train station on Railroad Avenue and proceed to Grand Avenue to the residence of Lester Waller. The marchers would then countermarch down Grand Avenue back to the railroad, ending at "Kurtz Hall" (the hotel). "All along the line of march, residences will be illuminated. There will also be a large and handsome banner raised in front of the hotel." Addresses were going to be made by Professor John E. Gill of Trenton, J. Alfred Judge of Windsor and all of the local candidates running for office. There was even a special train, leaving Trenton at about 7:30 "for the benefit of paraders." Lunch for all the participants was provided by the Ewing Township Republican Club.[64]

Celebrations such as this were not just Republican affairs. In 1912, it was the Democrats' turn. On the evening of October 18th, "an old fashioned Democratic flag pole raising" took place at the hotel and none other than Mayor Frederick W. Donnelly was scheduled to

---

[62] Trenton Evening Times, August 26, 1907.

[63] The Advance Guard of the City Invincibles were "the crack campaign marching club of the city" of Trenton, under the leadership of Captain Rutherford Havon. The following year they attended the inauguration of President Theodore Roosevelt.

[64] Trenton Times, October 20, 1904.

preside. The Democratic National Committee supplied Judge Robert Lincoln Dick of New York as the principal speaker. Other speakers at the exciting event were former Assemblyman Allan B. Walsh, who was now a candidate for Congress; Counsellor Erwin Marshall; Counselor William H. Geraghly; John Kearns, a candidate for the State Assembly; former Tax Receiver Andrew J. Berrien, now a candidate for County Clerk; and Sheriff Walter Madden.[65]

Once again, Winkler's Band provided musical entertainment. A large delegation was to arrive from Trenton shortly after eight o'clock in the evening. They were to be met by the band and escorted to the flag raising site by the hotel. Charles M. Donald, a New Yorker who had a "country residence" in Ewing Township, provided a buffet luncheon.[66]

By 1914, the Trenton Junction Hotel came under new ownership. Former Trenton Assessor Edward M. Reading, who already had a thriving hotel in Florence, New Jersey, purchased Kurtz's hotel. After some renovations, during the summer of 1914 the "Hotel Reading, formerly the Trenton Junction Hotel, having been renovated, [was] now prepared to serve meals." A Special Chicken Dinner was available on Sundays from 1 to 2:30p.m. for just 75¢![67]

Just as it was with Kurtz before, the Reading Hotel was considered the local "watering hole" for the residents of Trenton Junction, and the township at large. In July 1915, Reading was granted permission by the Mercer Court "...to conduct a wholesale liquor business in connection with his retail traded at Trenton Junction."[68] This business, however, was encroached upon by Edgar L. Kearns, a bottler of Trenton, and that interfered with Reading's profits. So, in August of that year, Reading filed a "bill in the Court of Chancery to restrain Kearns from continuing the sale of liquor" in Ewing Township. He alleged that

---

[65]   Trenton Evening Times, October 18, 1912.

[66]   Trenton Evening Times, October 18, 1912.

[67]   Trenton Evening Times, July 18, 1914. Seventy-five cents in 1914 is the equivalent of $17.75 in 2016.

[68]   Trenton Evening Times, July 10, 1915.

Kearns had a license to sell alcohol only in the city of Trenton, "...and when he disposes of his goods in Ewing Township he does so illegally. Reading asserted that he sells to people who were his customers and the business done by Kearns in the township has deprived him of large profit and gains."[69]

---

[69] Trenton Evening Times, August 27, 1915. The outcome of this case was not reported in the newspapers. It was overshadowed later that year by an $85,000 lawsuit brought against Kearns and his chauffeur after his chauffeur was involved in an auto accident with Dr. Louis H. Adler of Philadelphia.

Trenton Junction Hotel, circa 1900.

CHAPTER 6

"HE INDULGED NOT WISELY BUT TOO WELL"

IN THE DAYS BEFORE Trenton Junction hotel was around to provide a local place to drink, you could always take the train into Trenton to find a saloon. And that's just what Thomas Trainor and James Campbell did in April 1894. However, they enjoyed themselves a little too much, and on the morning of April 18th, Police Justice Solan fined them both: Trainor received a $10 fine but Campbell's fine was just $5.[70]

Four years later, James Murray, a Trenton Junction quarryman found himself a bit inebriated in Trenton. According to the *Trenton Evening Times*, Murray "came to town last night and indulged not wisely but too well in the liquids that induce a fighting spirit, and as a result he was locked up in the Central Station by Patrolman Higgins." He was granted a hearing and fined $2, "…which amount he failed to produce and he was remanded to await the arrival of a friend with the coins."[71]

One of the most notable arrests involving the sale of alcohol came in December 1906. Frank Roma was a wealthy Italian banker (and

---

[70] Trenton Evening Times, April 18, 1894.
[71] Trenton Evening Times, October 19, 1898.

barber) in Philadelphia[72]. Earlier in the year, a warrant was issued for Roma's arrest. On December 3rd, Roma found himself in the Mercer County Court where he was arraigned "...on a charge of selling liquor without a license, at a colony of Italian railroad employees, at Trenton Junction." An indictment was handed down by the grand jury and he pleaded not guilty. Released on bail, Roma's trial was set for December 17th.

According to the banking office, his arrest was "the result of spite work on the part of certain Trenton brewers, who had failed in getting the contract to supply the commissary with beer at the scene of the railroad operation."

The story goes that one Sunday, several weeks prior to Roma's arrest, a number of the Italian laborers in Trenton Junction, "...imbibed too freely and precipitated a fight. The brewers, it is declared, took advantage of this and, upon complaint being made, a warrant was issued for the arrest of Roma." Unfortunately, history does not record the result of his trial.[73]

In April 1929, during the height of Prohibition, the *Brooklyn Daily Eagle* ran an interesting story: A school of *drunken fish* led Federal agents to an illegal still near Trenton Junction: "A school of Fish, all elegantly soused, yesterday led to the discovery of a large still near Trenton Junction. State Policemen, Federal Agents, and a game warden were struck by the strange actions of the fish and soon investigation suspected them of being intoxicated." The police arrested two men and found a dozen vats containing 50,000 gallons of mash on the bank of the stream.[74]

---

[72] *The Tennessean*, the newspaper of Nashville, published an article in January 1907 in which it was stated that Frank Roma, was worth $500,000. Adjusting for inflation, that amount equates to $12,640,656 in 2016 dollars.

[73] The York Daily, December 5, 1906.

[74] Brooklyn Daily Eagle, April 11, 1929.

CHAPTER 7

BREAKERS OF THE LAW

IT WAS NOT JUST fish that were lawbreakers in Trenton Junction. On September 8, 1902, a half dozen cattle belonging to Mrs. Cooley broke their bonds and went on a rampage through Trenton Junction. "They ate half a dozen baskets of fruit and vegetables which had been left standing on the back porch of George Woodruff's home, destroyed a valuable tree, and many handsome plants. They also demolished H.H. Garwood's garden and committed many minor offenses" before they were discovered by neighbors and driven back to their pasture.[75]

A "wild dash to liberty" had occurred in 1902. The No. 51 express train for New York made a stop in Trenton Junction. Suddenly, one of the passengers, a prisoner of the United States Army, jumped from the train and "made a wild dash for liberty on the north side of the railroad." The prisoner was a soldier who had gone AWOL and he was being escorted by a "sergeant of artillery" from Allentown, Pennsylvania, to New York. The sergeant gave pursuit but was unable to catch up to the fleeing soldier. He fired several shots at him, but to no avail. The soldier "...ran back of the hotel across the vacant lots and through a corn field then crossed the Ewing Avenue into a thick

---

[75] Trenton Times, September 8, 1902.

woods owned by Levi Ackers and was soon lost to pursuit." Unable to recapture the escaped prisoner, the sergeant returned to Philadelphia.[76]

A more serious escape occurred in 1922. In April of that year, the New Jersey State Police had established their training school just west of Trenton Junction. Inmates from the State Prison in Trenton were working on the grounds of the training school. One of the inmates, Ralph Corra, made a daring escape ostensibly with the help of an accomplice. According to Joseph S. Hoff, the principal keeper of the State Prison, Corra slipped from the sight of his guards and made his get-away in an automobile that was waiting nearby. No trace of him was found.

Andrew Viscue, "a Trenton Junction Italian," was involved in a "chase" that saw him lose money twice! He took a ride into Trenton one night and "made the acquaintance of a couple of young women in a saloon" on North Willow Street by the Feeder Canal. At about 2 o'clock in the morning, Trenton Patrolman Cockran saw the two women "leaving the saloon on a run with Viscue in pursuit." Cockran joined in the pursuit, chasing after the threesome as they ran up Willow Street. Behind the Reading Station, he caught up with Viscue, but the women got away. Viscue accused the women of having some money that belonged to him. Now the City of Trenton was going to have its share of Viscue's money because Judge Jackson fined him $5.00![77]

In cities, unsuspecting people like Mr. Viscue were known to have their money stolen. However, in the countryside it was oftentimes chickens that were stolen. In December 1898, William Thackeray, whose farm was on the southern end of Trenton Junction, raised chickens. Sometime during the night of December 16th, his hen house was "entered and looted" and his chickens were "dressed for market" in a nearby stable. Approximately fifty chickens were taken to the stable

---

[76]   Trenton Times, September 30, 1902.

[77]   Trenton Times, September 3, 1902.

where they were "stuck and picked in the usual manner." Somehow, the thieves accomplished this very quietly as Thackeray was unaware anything was amiss until he entered the barn early the next morning.[78]

Burglars broke into the Trenton Junction Hotel and the Post Office in April 1904 and stole about $15 worth of stamps, a small amount of money and two quarts of whiskey. The newspaper was good enough to clarify that "the stamps and money were taken from the post office and the whiskey was stolen from Kurtz's hotel."[79] Later that year, a dispute broke out between Justice of the Peace Alfred Jerauld and Joseph Arnold, both of Trenton Junction. Jerauld had written an article in the Sunday Times Advertiser in which he charged Arnold with using a tent that belonged to the St. Alban's Episcopal Mission in Trenton Junction for personal use "...as a covering for his cabbage patch." Arnold took offense at this and demanded an apology. He insisted that the wind blew the tent down and that "as a member of the congregation of St. Alban's Mission, he took care of it" and spread it over his cabbages to dry it. When Jerauld refused to apologize, Arnold formally complained, charging Jerauld with being "a common nuisance" and a hearing was scheduled to be held before Justice of the Peace Reading. While the outcome of the hearing was not reported, it is interesting to note that the cabbage story was covered as far away as Rochester, New York in the *Democrat and Chronicle*![80]

This was not the first time that "Squire Jerauld" had gotten into trouble. In November 1893 "the Birmingham Justice of the Peace" was on trial at Mercer Court for extortion. The charge was proffered by Mrs. Mary Fenreu, also of Trenton Junction. Her son Thomas was arrested and taken before Squire Jerauld for trial. Jerauld imposed a fine of $130 for disorderly conduct in Lincoln Park, a fine which Thomas failed to pay. "Two weeks later [Thomas] was arrested for threatening language to Jonathan Howell, and a fine of $5 was imposed and paid.

---

[78] The [Philadelphia] Times, December 17, 1898.
[79] Trenton Times, April 27, 1904.
[80] Trenton Times, November 8, 1904; Democrat and Chronicle (Rochester, NY). November 12, 1904.

He was also required to give $100 bail to keep the peace and pay $1.60 for costs." The issue was with the $1.60 court costs. Fenreu's lawyer, Edward Evans, said that there was no law empowering a justice of the peace to impose that fee in this type of case. While Evans believed the fee was not imposed with any intent to extort money unlawfully, Mrs. Fenreu took Jerauld to court anyway, though the case was most likely dismissed.[81]

John J. Ford, a constable with the Trenton Police Department, made his way to Trenton Junction one morning early in July, 1896. He was there to arrest John Strause, a local resident, on a warrant for petty larceny issued by Squire Reading. The complainant, James J. Mount of Ewing Township, alleged that Strause had stolen from him a pair of hair clippers, valued at $4.50, and two razors, valued at $5. When Constable Ford made the arrest, Strause "protested his innocence so violently that Ford was obliged to apply the handcuffs." Strause realized that resistance was futile and confessed. "The goods were secured from his house and he was brought to Trenton and committed to county jail."[82]

Theodore Ivans was a local Trenton Junction milkman and in June 1904, he failed the lactometer test. A lactometer is a device used for testing the purity of milk. It's a simple device, consisting of a cylindrical glass tube filled with mercury. A second tube has scale markings. The lactometer is simply dipped in milk and the point up to which it sinks shows the milk's purity. It sinks less in milk than water because milk is denser than water. If the tube sinks too far, the milk has been mixed with water and is not pure.[83]

Ivans found himself in the City District Court in Trenton. He, and

---

[81] Trenton Times, November 10, 1893. In 1890, Alfred Jerauld and his wife Mary moved into the house on the southwest corner of Ewing and Grand Avenues (now West Upper Ferry Road and Grand Avenue) and lived there until February 1909 when they moved across from the train station near Carrigg Avenue. Alfred Jerauld died on April 29, 1909.

[82] Trenton Evening Times, July 7, 1896.

[83] http://www.articlesfactory.com/articles/business/how-to-check-milk-purity-using-lactometer-milk-testing-equipment.html.

Princeton milkman Peter Campbell, were prosecuted by Theodore Backes of the Attorney General's Office for violating the state health code and peddling milk that "was not up to the required standard." They were fined $50 each.[84]

In 1906, Charlie Saltman of Trenton Junction hired Bernard Trainer, Jr., of South Broad Street in Trenton, to move some of his furniture. As can be expected, it did not go well:

> Trainor claimed he made a bargain to haul a few chairs and some other goods for Saltman and said that when he got to the house Saltman had a half a ton of coal and enough other stuff to make up two loads. Trainor refused to cart the goods for the price agreed upon. Saltman, he said, waited until he had the coal on the wagon and then refused to pay an extra price. Trainor then took the coal and Saltman had him arrested. The coal was finally dumped at the police station, pending a disposition of the suit. Judge Harris... decided that Saltman had no case against [Trainor] and told him to move the coal from the station house. 'I lost a day's wages, paid for an extra wagon and now I got to pay for the moving of the coal again. Where do I get off?' retorted Saltman. There was no answer.[85]

A law suit over money was brought against Charles Reed who refused to repay a $50 loan. In September 1897, Mary Sutton of Spring Street in Trenton sued Reed, who was a night watchman on the Philadelphia and Pennsylvania Railroad. A few years earlier, in 1893, Reed borrowed $50 from Sutton, giving as security "a note for six months on his household goods," signed by Reed and his wife. At the end of the six months, he refused to repay the loan, however in February 1897 he paid her $2 interest. Charles Reed claimed that Mary Sutton owed him for eleven weeks' board at $4 per week, totaling $44. Sutton, of course, denied the claim. [86]

---

[84] Trenton Times, June 14, 1904. $50 at that time is the equivalent of $1,289.86 in 2016 dollars.

[85] Trenton Evening Times, November 12, 1906.

[86] Trenton Evening Times, September 16, 1897.

CHAPTER 8

BOOGIE MEN AT THE JUNCTION

IN JULY 1899, THE Boogie Man came to Trenton Junction. Or, more accurately, the Boogie *Men*, being as there were two of them. Who they were and why they were there is a mystery that is nearly 125 years old. They were two quiet, unassuming individuals who "badly frightened" the citizens of Trenton Junction.

"The residents of...Trenton Junction, the capital city's pretty little suburb to the northward, are beginning to breath freely again and stay out of doors after dark, all of which means that the 'boogie men' of the past week have disappeared and instead of their mysterious visits, peace and quietness abounds as of yore." The two men suddenly appeared and caused all kinds of rumors to circulate concerning who they were and why they came to the Junction.

"These individuals, whose unexplained presence kept the whole community guessing, were two well-dressed young strangers who made daily trips to and from Trenton, and whose purpose, if any, in so doing went out into the great unknown with them when they left the town the other evening, bound no one knows where."

The two men arrived in Trenton sometime during the first week of July. They registered at the United States Hotel as "A.J. Patterson, Philadelphia" and "F.S. Campbell, Washington." The owner of the hotel "...did not inquire into the pedigree or ancestral history of his guests. They paid their bills promptly and presented every appearance of respectability and honesty and that was all he required."

The other guests at the hotel were quite happy to have the strangers there as they "proved the ideal of good fellowship, were always ready with an interesting story, and treated to moxie, soda, etc., when their turn came like noblemen to the manor born." No one noticed that they left town each day until "from the Junction came vague rumors of their strange behavior."

According to the *Trenton Times*, "the natives were mystified and alarmed" by the daily visits of the two men, "who offered no explanation of their object." They rarely went to Kurtz's hotel (it is assumed for meals) and they spent most of their time watching the arrival and departure of trains and "inspecting from the outside the farm houses and cottages of the neighborhood." It was as if they were casing the joint!

This, naturally, led to wild speculation, as reported by the local paper. "Land sharks, by gum," said one resident, "hunting for a town site ter invest in; keep a stiff upper lip and a high price on the farm medder if they want ter buy it."

"Confidence men, sure as yer born," claimed another, "got a gold brick or some mine stock for sale, better stay in at nights fer awhile, anyhow."

"Naw, yer all wrong," claimed the agent at the train station, "them sports is private detectives watching fer some escaping bank cashier, or sumpin' else."

The daily trips of the two men and their mysterious actions aroused the suspicions of Joseph Martindale, the railroad conductor, with whom they often rode. He instructed the express messenger on the train to carry the "burglar-proof safe in his vest pocket until further notice."

No one was immune to the jitters these strangers were bringing to Trenton Junction. Freeholder George Howell "put up scarecrows all over his farm and slept with one eye open and a corn knife beneath his pillow." James Force, a lawyer, kept both hands on his pocketbook and put up a bunk in his Trenton office so he would not have to return home until the coast was clear.

Squire Jerauld "took his rest in the day time and guarded his hen roost with a shot gun after dark. 'Can't afford to take no chances with them Inter-State fair prize winners," said he, with an admiring glance at the big lazy chickens."

John Callahan was the railroad section boss. He carried a few "signal torpedoes" with him in case of emergency. Matthews, the blacksmith, "worked overtime in beating plow shares and pruning hooks, into swords and spears." Even Constable Winkler, Ewing Township Constable, "built a lockup in his barn, and shadowed the pair whenever the sun was bright enough to make a shadow." The whole village was up in arms, "especially the youngsters, from six months on down, and there's no telling what might have happened had the 'boogies' continued their naughty tricks."

Then one night the two strangers packed their bags and left! They told hotel manager McCarthy "…that a company they were to represent here did not materialize, and took their departure, after bidding everybody [at the hotel] an affectionate farewell. They said they would return in two weeks, and as for them Trenton Junction fellows, 'the boogie man will get 'em if they don't watch out!'"[87]

---

[87] Trenton Times, July 12, 1899.

CHAPTER 9

ROBBERS, BURGLARS, TRAMPS AND THIEVES!

Early in the morning of October 3, 1893, the residence of Peter W. Crozer at Trenton Junction "was entered by burglars...and goods to the amount of $400 were taken." The burglars made their entry through a front window and, after looting the lower floor, they went upstairs, "taking any article of value upon which they could lay their hands."

Chief McChasney of Ewing Police was called and his detectives took over the case. Two men were reported during the evening "skulking along the railroad track near the house," but no identification was made and no clues obtained.

The burglars made off with "three overcoats, a plush smoking-jacket, under coats and pants of clothing, as well as a gold watch and chain, and several dollars in money...together with the silver on the table in the dining room and some plated spoons."

The only evidence left behind at the scene was a number of burned matches, found in different parts of the house. They were apparently used to find the stolen items.

An arrest was made on October 12 by Philadelphia Detectives. Charles Bender, alias Charles Mack was one of the men who robbed

Crozer's home. He was caught in Philadelphia "while disposing of the proceeds of a robbery recently committed in Norristown, Pennsylvania." Charles White, alias Charles Wallace, was the other burglar. Both were young men "but hardened criminals" with a rap sheet, according to the Philadelphia police.

Charles White was extradited to New Jersey and on the afternoon of November 13th, stood trial at the Mercer Court in Trenton. "The prisoner, a pallid, delicate, black whiskered, gentlemanly looking fellow" was defended by Frank Lee and Frank S. Katzenbach, Jr. Assistant Prosecutor W. Holt Apgar conducted the case on behalf of the State.

Pete Crozer testified that "...his house at Trenton Junction was entered by burglars one night in October last and a gold watch and chain, a lot of plated ware, some clothing and a case of drawing instruments [were] stolen. The goods were valued at $250. He said the burglars entered by forcing the parlor window."

In a strange twist, Charles White wore "a suit of the stolen clothes" at the trial! Peter Crozer's son, Louis, testified that the coat the prisoner was wearing in court belonged to the witness, and that the prisoner's trousers were owned by the witness' brother. Louis had earlier accompanied Detective Pilger of the Ewing Police Department to Abrams' Pawn Shop on Ninth Street in Philadelphia where he recovered his father's watch. Pilger testified that while at Philadelphia Police Headquarters, he had a conversation with Charles White who told Pilger that a party named Mack actually "did the job" and that he (White) pawned the items for him. He was found guilty and sentenced to ten years in the State Prison for robbing Peter Crozier's residence.[88]

Charles Bender (alias Mack) was not extradited to New Jersey. He was, however, tried in Pennsylvania for the Norristown robbery and, on December 6, 1893, was sentenced to five years in the state penitentiary.[89]

---

[88] Trenton Times, October 3 and 12 1893; November 11 and 13, 1893; Philadelphia Inquirer, November 14, 1893.

[89] The Allentown Leader (Allentown, Pennsylvania), December 6, 1893.

In April 1903 another burglary was reported in Trenton Junction. Thieves entered the cellars of Jean Rittenhouse and John Carrigg. At Carrigg's house, they stole a number of chickens and at Rittenhouse's they helped themselves to food. After robbing and dining, they stole a horse and wagon from John Kurtz's hotel and drove to Trenton. The horse and wagon were later found on Stuyvesant Avenue, but the thieves got away.[90]

A lethal robbery occurred in 1894. In the morning of June 5th, the body of Trenton Junction resident Edward Powers was found in the Trenton basin of the canal "in a badly decomposed state." Coroner Bowers ordered its removal to the morgue where an autopsy was to be performed.

On May 28, 1894, Powers, a retired veteran, left Trenton Junction for Trenton, to work out arrangements regarding his pension. Along the way, he stopped at the Howard Cycle Company to make a payment on a bicycle for one of his grandchildren. While there, he foolishly "exhibited quite a large sum of money" and when his body was found, the money was missing. "Over one eye was found a large bruise, but the skin is not broken. The vicinity of the basin is a rendezvous for tramps, and it is thought that Powers may have been robbed and his body thrown overboard. Nothing was found about his person but a return ticket between Trenton Junction and [Trenton], dated May 28. The supposition is that he has been in the water since then."[91]

Coroner Bowers was called back to Trenton Junction by H.T. Herbert. A body of an unknown dead man had been found at Jones'

---

[90] Trenton Times, April 8, 1903.
[91] Trenton Times, June 5, 1894.

Barracks, just up the hill from the Birmingham section of the Junction. The body was brought to Murphy's Morgue in Trenton, but no identification is known to have been made.[92] A more bizarre mystery occurred in October 1903 when the *Trenton Times* reported that "Coroner Rogers has been unable as yet to learn anything concerning the human foot found yesterday at Trenton Junction"![93]

The train station in the early years of the century was not without its problems, as well. Tramps and "shady characters" would be seen milling about. On Valentine's Day 1904, a girl from Trenton was visiting friends in Trenton Junction. That evening, she lost a valuable gold watch while waiting in the station for a train back home. It was believed that it was stolen by some of the "rough men who frequent the place."[94]

Just a few months later, in late July 1904, a local Trenton Junction woman took matters into her own hands when she was plagued by a milk thief. Unbeknownst to the thief, she replaced her cow with a rather angry bull. She was given credit for her scheme "which served as detective, conviction and punishment all at once!"[95]

In keeping with the milk theme, Joseph Atchley, a local Trenton milkman, caught a man climbing into his Trenton Junction home in mid-October 1905. Mrs. Atchley was in the sitting room with their child and Mr. Atchley was asleep on the couch when she saw a man looking through a window. "She kept quiet to await developments,

---

92 Trenton Evening Times, March 30, 1896.

93 Trenton Times, October 21, 1903.

94 Trenton Times, February 16, 1904.

95 Trenton Times, July 29, 1904.

realizing that the man believed her to be alone with the child." When he tried to enter the house, she called for her husband. He chased the intruder through the yard, "minus his hat, coat and shoes...and would have caught him had not the rascal been small enough to crawl through a hole in the fence—a hole too narrow to admit Mr. Atchley's portly form." Atchley tried to follow but "was caught fast" and before he could work himself free, the intruder had disappeared. [96]

On December 29, 1905, three Trenton Junction houses were robbed "...and even children [were] relieved of holiday gifts." George Woodruff, John Matthews and Joseph Arnold, Jr, were victims of a gang of robbers that made their escape by train. The three houses were broken into and ransacked and plundered of goods and Christmas gifts. No trace of the thieves was found and it was believed that they made their escape on one of Reading freight and coal trains that often passed through during the night at a slow speed because of the steep grade.

In each case, the houses were entered through a window that had inadvertently been left unlocked. "The biggest haul was made at the Arnold home. Mr. Arnold lost two coats, an over and under garment, a pair of gold spectacles, an initial cane (a Christmas present from his wife) and a pair of kid gloves. Mrs. Arnold lost a coat, a part of a new suit and a set of marten furs. The children were relieved of a lot of candy which they had left on a table. It is thought the thieves were frightened away before completing their work for they did not disturb some silverware and a lot of valuable brick-a-brac. At the home of Mr. Woodruff, a child's purse containing about one dollar, a boy's watch and a gold pin—all Christmas presents—were stolen. From Mr. Matthews the thieves got an overcoat and numerous small articles."

---

[96] Trenton Times, October 25, 1905.

The Trenton Police were notified and Detectives Pilger and Clancy were assigned the case, but to no avail.[97]

In 1909, one of the "boldest robberies and attempts at murder ever reported" in the Trenton Junction area occurred in the early morning of November 9th, "when a desperate negro robbed nearly three score men and finally shot one seriously who caught him in the act." Nearly 100 Italian laborers were living in the railroad camp near the Philadelphia and Reading Railroad station in Trenton Junction. According to the *Asbury Park Press*, they lived in a long, wooden shanty and it was known that "…they keep their savings in their bunks. Many of them are also known to be armed, for fear of robbers."

John Giacomo, the man who was shot, said that a "powerfully built black man" broke into the shanty by forcing open a door. "With a shotgun in one hand, he stole quietly along the various bunks and helped himself to whatever cash or valuables he could find. In some of the rooms there were several men sleeping…" He had robbed about 60 of the men without awakening them; however, when he reached Giacomo's bunk he made a noise. Giacomo woke up and saw the man rifling through his pockets. He immediately jumped out of his bunk and grappled with him. The burglar "…drew back and pointed the gun at him. He pulled the trigger and the victim fell to the floor. A second load of shot entered his back as he fell."

The report of the gun woke up the others. The burglar fled and the men chased after him and tried to surround him, but he held them back with his gun while he ran down the railroad tracks. Just then, an eastbound coal train came along and it was believed that the burglar jumped on the train and made his escape.[98]

---

[97] Trenton Times, December 30, 1905.

[98] Asbury Park Press, November 9, 1909.

In 1917, there was a bit of excitement at the hotel, across from the train station. Edward Reading, the new proprietor of the Trenton Junction Hotel, and his wife were chased by one of their employees, Antonio Bazowiski, who was brandishing a loaded revolver and threatening to kill their servant girl, Annie Kalensky.

Reading was able to catch the man and held him until Constable DeCosta of the Ewing Police arrived to place him under arrest. He was held in the Central Police Station by Squire Kelsey under $500 bail. It turned out that he was on probation for three years after having served part of an 18 month sentence for criminally assaulting a 14-year-old girl in Ewing Township.[99]

Often, at the turn of the century, rail lines would attract tramps. In 1897, it was reported that "…the Trenton Junction bands of tramps have been particularly difficult to handle. They have been robbing many of the country residents and committing all sorts of depredations, and so bold have they become that girls have been warned not to go bicycling unescorted on the river path."[100]

Things were not much better after the turn of the century. In 1911, for example, two tramps stopped at Ewing Crossing and attempted to cook a piece of meat on the watchman's stove. When the watchman, Giuseppe Criciana returned to his cabin, a fight ensued and the watchman was badly battered by the tramps.[101]

Tramps did not only go after the well-off; they sometimes went after one another. William Boone was a hermit living on the edge of a swamp near the road to Trenton Junction. He liked to tell the story

---

[99] Trenton Evening Times, December 14, 1917.

[100] Trenton Evening Times, April 16, 1897.

[101] Reading Times (Pennsylvania), March 13, 1911. Ewing Crossing was the next stop after Trenton Junction heading north. It was located at the spot where Scotch Road intersected with the rail line, not far from the current Upper Ferry Road and Glenroc Shopping Center.

of how a "professional tramp" lost his beard and pretended to lose his life in order to win a wager of one dollar at Boone's shack.

Boone could read and write and, in fact, spent most of his time doing just that—reading and occasionally writing to rural newspapers. He was also a recent convert to Christian Science. Now there was another "wanderer" who was affectionately known as "Dan" who had long suffered from heart disease. Or so he said. And because he "said," he "received food and clothing from locals who sympathized with him on account of his ailment." Boone often helped Dan out, in an attempt to convert him over to Christian Science.

According to the story, Dan, "in the course of a heated argument with his would-be benefactor, exclaimed, according to Boone: 'I don't believe no such rot and I am ready to bet my beard that it ain't true!'" Dan then took a kerosene lamp, unscrewed it and poured the kerosene all over his "grizzly hirsute adornment." Boone was so startled by this he was unable to protest "as the tramp struck a match and held it at arm's length while he cried: 'I dare you to try to save my beard by any of your magic religion, or whatever you call it. Darn me if I believe that story about the Almighty saving people in the fiery furnace, or any other rot that the new-fangled sects pretend to believe!'"

Then, according to Boone, Dan "brought the burning match to the point of his beard and in an instant his face was ablaze. With cool calculation, the tramp then plunged his head into a tin basin that he had filed with water a few moments before…The water extinguished the flames that had burned off the beard."

"'I might as well be a good looking stiff,' declared Dan, 'now I am going to croak. The heart disease has got me for fair. A gypsy woman up the road told me that I would die before noon if I didn't cross the palm of her hand with silver. The only piece of silver is this—the first real dollar I have seen in ten years—and I bet you this identical cartwheel that I will be dead as a door nail in an hour. Begin your mysterious healing humbuggery right now, and I bet this cartwheel that you can't save me.'"

Dan the tramp then sprawled "full length on a couch in the kitchen and proceeded to die, judging from his appearance. In a few minutes,

Boone was convinced that the tramp was lifeless and started in search of a coroner, leaving on a little table beside the dead man two silver dollars, the one that the tramp had wagered on his own death and the other placed there by Boone as evidence of his faith in Christian Science. Returning in a few minutes Boone found that the tramp had disappeared, taking the two silver dollars with him."[102]

---

[102] The Tennessean (Nashville, Tennessee). November 10, 1910.

CHAPTER 10

HAVE GUN, WILL SHOOT

IN MODERN DAY POLITICS, gun control has become a hotly contested issue. While that may not be very surprising, what may be surprising is that the issue is not new. On November 20, 1905, an article ran in the *Trenton Times* in which Judge Harris of Trenton is said to have declared that he "will punish all who carry pistols."

Judge Harris was reacting to the arrest of Joseph Salvatore, an Italian laborer working on the railroad in Trenton Junction. Salvatore was arrested by Patrolman Willard Kelly "for being drunk and flourishing a revolver on North Broad Street [in Trenton] Saturday night." Harris fined him $35 for carrying the revolver and $10 for disorderly conduct.

At the hearing in police court, Harris declared: "I mean to stop the carrying of revolvers in this community and to enforce the state law against such crime. Some persons believe they have a privilege to carry concealed weapons but I want them to know that they have not and that the practice must cease. The lives of too many people are endangered by the promiscuous use of weapons."[103]

One person who should never have had access to a weapon was Charles Helmuth. On the morning of January 22, 1896, Justice of the Peace Mills committed Helmut to the county jail in default of $300 bail

---

[103] Trenton Times, November 20, 1905.

on a charge of atrocious assault and battery. Helmut was employed in the Trenton Junction control tower on the Philadelphia and Reading Railroad. He had been drinking and his boss, Daniel Carrigg, replaced him for the day. Infuriated and drunk, Helmuth went to Carrigg's house and got into a scuffle with his boss. He pointed a revolver at Carrigg and threatened to shoot him.

Helmuth would be in the news again, exactly six months later. On June 22, 1896, he was arrested and "lodged in the county jail" after he "...created consternation in the quiet town of Trenton Junction."

According to the *Philadelphia Inquirer*, during the evening of June 21, Helmuth

> ...ran amuck through the quiet town with a revolver in each hand, shooting right and left, causing pedestrians to seek places of safety. In his erratic course he stopped at the home of Daniel Carrigg, section foreman of the Philadelphia and Reading Railroad, and called him to the door. After a few minutes' conversation of a friendly character, he drew a revolver and commenced shooting at Carrigg and other members of his family. His aim was poor and no one was injured. Charles Salimer and Thomas Shelby, employees of the Reading Road, who were passing at the time, overpowered the frenzied man, but he escaped and remained in hiding until today.[104]

Two weeks before this incident, Helmuth became angry at a neighbor and drew a revolver on him. These three incidents "...give rise to the belief that he is deranged."

Unfortunately for Frank Frascella and John Connelly, they learned of the dangers of guns a bit too late. John Connelly was an assistant "tramp catcher" working for the Reading Railroad and Frank "Spitz" Frascella was a Trenton cab driver. Normally, Frascella would wait at the Reading Station on North Warren Street in Trenton once a week to meet the train bringing immigrants from steamships in New York.

---

[104] Philadelphia Inquirer, June 22, 1896.

He was Italian, well-educated and knew how to direct the wandering immigrants when they got off the trains. "All of the foreigners would have notes written in English or tags on their clothes written in the same language, so they could be directed to different places in [Trenton]. Finally a few of the cabmen began to charge exorbitant prices and the matter was brought to the attention of the county authorities. Squire Manfred Naar, who is chief of the Reading Staff of Detectives advised Frascella to drive to the Trenton Junction Station and meet the immigrant train there instead."

On the evening of April 4, 1910, Frascella arrived early. He and Connelly were joined by Special Officer Roy Acord of the Reading Railway Detective Force and sat on a baggage truck at the station while waiting for the immigrant train to arrive.

Acord "...was sitting in front of the Trenton Junction Train Station with Frascella and Connelly. I displayed a revolver which I had borrowed from Ambrose Miller, the telegraph operator at the Trenton Junction Station, some days ago. Connelly took the gun from me" and, thinking the gun was not loaded, proceeded to examine it. As he was showing it to Frascella, Connelly remarked, "How would you like to get a load from this one?" Suddenly, there was a loud bang and Frascella fell to the station platform with a bullet through his heart!

Connelly was terrified. Acord said that "as soon as Connelly saw Frascella drop he ran away and I gave pursuit. He ran around the station and before I could catch up with him he turned the weapon upon himself and fired, dying by his own act."

Doctor Charles H. Waters, one of the doctors employed by the railroad, was called to the station and he pronounced the men dead. Connelly's funeral was held on April 7th from the home of his widowed mother. Burial was in St. Mary's Cemetery in Trenton. Frascella's funeral was held the following day.[105]

---

[105] Trenton Evening Times, April 5, 1910; Wilkes-Barra Evening News (Wilkes-Barre, Pennsylvania), April 6, 1910; The Wilkes-Barra Record (Wilkes-Barre, Pennsylvania), April 6, 1910; Nevada State Journal, April 6, 1910; Trenton Evening Times, April 7, 1910.

Sadly, this was not the only accidental tragedy with a loaded gun. Three years earlier, in August 1907, eight-year-old Helen Downes of Trenton Junction, along with her brother, were visiting the LaRue family in Pennington, New Jersey. Helen and the two little LaRue girls went upstairs to play. "A loaded single-barrel shotgun, standing in the corner of the room, was knocked over and discharged. The load struck Helen, tearing off the top of her head."

Doctor William Radcliff was summoned, but death was instantaneous. Coroner Hulitt was notified, and he decided that an inquest would not be necessary. It was his opinion that Helen's death was accidental. He released her body and she was taken home to Trenton Junction.[106]

In the evening of October 31, 1915, nineteen-year-old Benjamin Fort and eighteen-year-old Norman Thackeray, along with their friends Edward Grover, Herbert Scammell, Clifford Jones, Edward and Anthony Goetz and John Tyman, were celebrating Hallowe'en. Thackeray and Fort and their gang of friends, with the permission of Fred Manning, were pulling an old wagon from Manning's blacksmith shop. As they reached the road, they suddenly heard a voice from the darkness call out, "Halt!" Before they had time to comply, a shot was fired, "entering the legs and feet of Fort and Thackeray." Two men were seen standing in the shadow of a large tree near the blacksmith shop, but they disappeared after the shooting.

Fort and Thackeray were helped by their friends to the Grover home. Doctor E.B. Allen, a former resident of Trenton Junction, was called and he tended to their wounds. Their injuries were quite painful—about six shots were taken from Fort's legs and about 40 from Thackeray's. Anthony Goetz, too, it was later learned, had been hit in his left wrist. "While the youths are said to be getting along as well as can be expected their condition is none too favorable, and just what the outcome of their injuries will be is problematical."

Assistant Prosecutor English and County Detective Kirkham were investigating the strange case. As the boys had been given permission

[106] Trenton Evening Times, August 12, 1907; The Scranton Republican (Scranton, Pennsylvania), August 13, 1907.

to take the old wagon, and they were doing no damage, the authorities were at a loss as to a motive.

By November 5th, the entire village of Trenton Junction was in an uproar. The police had not yet made any arrests. Finally, Alvin A. Temple was arrested and charged with the shooting. He was held on $2,000 bail by Justice Naar while awaiting the decision of the Grand Jury. Temple ran a saw mill at Trenton Junction and he made a practice of shooting cats, dogs, and chickens which happened to wander onto his property.

On January 14, 1916, Temple was brought before Judge Marshall in Mercer Court. Marshall bitterly denounced the several people who wrote to him asking that he impose a "penal sentence" on Mr. Temple. The judge made it known that he did not appreciate such letters and criticized the petitioners from the bench in open court. The judge stated that he could "easily understand the writing of letters for clemency as a feeling of humanity, but failed to understand a cold-blooded demand for a penal sentence."

Judge Marshall did sentence Temple to pay a fine of $150 and costs, amounting to $244.68. Temple entered a plea of guilty to atrocious assault and battery. He confessed that he had indeed "fired the contents of a shotgun into a crowd of young men whom he believed were playing pranks on him. It later developed that the men did not touch anything belonging to Temple, neither were they on his property."

Not satisfied with the fine imposed upon Alvin Temple, on February 18, 1916, Benjamin Fort and Norman Thackeray filed suit in the Mercer Circuit Court for $5,000 damages each. Because the plaintiffs were minors, the suits were brought in the names of their fathers, and W. Holt Apgar represented them in court.

"Temple was not given notice of the suit in the ordinary way by the service of a summons, but was taken into custody on a *capias* and cast into jail until he furnished a bond of $1,000 to insure his appearance to answer the suits."[107]

---

[107] Trenton Evening Times, November 2 & 5, 1915; Trenton Evening Times, January 14, 1916; Trenton Evening Times, February 18, 1916. A *capias* is a writ ordering the arrest of a named person.

On June 26, 1921, another shooting occurred, right in the heart of Trenton Junction.

Charles Delmonico moved to Trenton Junction in 1898. Since 1909, he was employed by the Agasote Millboard Company—the original name of the Homasote Company— as a blacksmith. He and his wife Angeline were the parents of eight children and made their home on Grand Avenue. Mrs. Mary Sposato and Bruno D'Angelo, a laborer employed in building the new concrete road on Grand Avenue, also rented space in the double-frame house. However, in mid-June, 1921, Delmonico evicted both D'Angelo and Mrs. Sposato because "D'Angelo made threats against his life and the lives of members of his family, and [because] Mrs. Sposato owed him $20."

Allegedly, Bruno D'Angelo, who was 23 years old, was infatuated with Delmonico's 15-year-old daughter, Mary. To complicate matters, Mrs. Spostato, with whom D'Angelo lived, attempted several times to convince Mary to elope with D'Angelo, "pointing out that her tender years need be no bar to marriage." Mary rebuffed these amorous advances, and each time D'Angelo grew more enraged. Eventually, he began to make threats and "…frequently boasted that he would get the girl dead or alive" and recently attempted to slash Mary and two of her sisters with a razor. The attack on the children was thwarted by their mother who "…slammed a door in the face of the wood-be lover and prevented his entrance into the house." Fearing for his safety and that of his family, Charles began carrying a gun.

Tragedy struck shortly after 3 o'clock on the afternoon of June 26, 1921. Charles was sitting on his front porch talking with his friend Fred Traviline when a trolley came down the street. And who should hop off the trolley in front of Delmonico's house but Bruno D'Angelo. Before heading to Trenton Junction, D'Angelo allegedly told friends that he was heading back to the house to retrieve a watch and chain he had left there.

By the time Charles Delmonico had gotten up and walked to the front of his porch, his wife Angelina was already ordering D'Angelo off the property. At this point, Delmonico asked him why he was there and he said that D'Angleo made a move "as if to draw a gun." Delmonico drew his gun and, firing first, shot Bruno D'Angelo through the head and chest.

D'Angelo collapsed to the ground, killed instantly. Leaving the dead man lying in the street, Delmonico went back into the house, changed his clothing, washed his face and hands and then boarded a trolley, came to Trenton where he surrendered himself to the police." He gave a complete confession, and told the story of D'Angelo's untoward advances against his young daughter.

Delmonico pleaded self-defense and his case was taken up by the Grand Jury in July. While it will never be known for sure just what Bruno D'Angelo's intention was, when county authorities visited the scene of the crime later that afternoon, they searched his clothing and discovered a razor, a stiletto, and a loaded revolver.[108]

---

[108] Trenton Evening Times, June 27, 1921; Winston-Salem Journal (Winston-Salem, North Carolina), June 29, 1921; Kingsport Times (Kingsport, Tennessee), July 2, 1921; Trenton Evening Times, July 6 & 8, 1921. Did Delmonico win his case? The newspapers decided not to let us know!

CHAPTER 11

ASSAULT & BATTERY

IT IS SOMETIMES BELIEVED that crime in the late nineteenth and early twentieth centuries in rural areas was rare—that most crime occurred in the more densely populated urban areas. While that may or may not be accurate, it has been shown in earlier chapters that there was crime—at times violent crime—in the farming community of Trenton Junction. Armed Robberies, burglaries, and shootings, while not necessarily common, did, in fact, occur. And so, too, did crimes of assault and battery.

Assault, defined as "any willful attempt or threat to inflict injury upon the person of another" and battery, "the actual unlawful, physical contact with another" are, of course, without justification or excuse.[109] The relatively rare occurrence of assault and battery in Trenton Junction usually resulted in the arrest and conviction of the perpetrator.

The earliest newspaper account of an assault appeared in the October 8, 1886 edition of the *Trenton Times*. The previous June, Sarah Ely attended a picnic held in Lincoln Park, across from the Pennsylvania

---

[109] Black's Law Dictionary. Fifth edition. West Publishing Company, St. Paul, Minn. 1979.

& Reading Railroad Station. She decided it was time to leave, so she proceeded to walk home along the train tracks.

> William Hall, a colored man...followed her up the track and told her he was going home with her. 'No, you are not,' replied Sarah. [Hall] insisted and put his arms around her. She pushed him away. He then made improper proposals to her. She told him he should do nothing of the kind. He then followed her and kept hitting her on the back with something. He must have done it with a knife or some sharp instrument, as the next morning she found that the dress had been cut in a good many places. The night watchman then came up and asked what was the matter. When she told him he told her to go on and if the man bothered her again he would be on hand. The whole affair happened less than a hundred yards from the station, where there were a number of people waiting for a train.[110]

William Hall was arrested and placed on trial for the assault. Edward Voorhees, who testified that he was at the picnic, was called on behalf of the defendant. He testified that he saw William Hall go from the train station up behind her, but he never saw him put his hands on her and he did not hear any arguing.

Hall testified on his own behalf, claiming that Sarah "...said something to him [and Voorhees] at the depot about somebody going home with her. Voorhees would not go and he started up the track, thinking he would go with her. He only went a little way and then turned back without saying anything to her."

George Howell, who had his farm in Trenton Junction, was called as a character witness on behalf of William Hall. He testified to his good character, stating that Hall had worked for him on the farm several times. Hall was found guilty of assault and was committed to jail for 60 days.[111]

---

[110] Trenton Times, October 8, 1886.
[111] Trenton Times, October 8, 1886.

Four years later, in September 1890, Mary McCue was attacked "in the Swamp" near Trenton Junction sometime "late Saturday night or early Sunday morning." Although she was "not as badly hurt as was at first supposed, she had several bad cuts in the face and neck, however, and will require medical attendance for some time." Thomas "Skip" Weldran was arrested and charged with the attack. Justice of the Peace Matheson committed him to jail on a charge of atrocious assault and battery.[112]

Another victim of a knife attack was Charles Hunt. In 1904, John Gretzo and Charles Hunt, two farm hands working for Howard Simpkins, were hanging out, drinking hard cider. The two men got into a quarrel about who should take care of a horse on the farm. Gretzo pulled a knife and slashed Hunt across the face "...in such a manner that Dr. Allen was called and eight stitches were required to draw the wound together." Gretzo fled to Trenton on the 1:53 train that afternoon. The police had not yet arrested him when Hunt declined to press charges.[113]

In March 1905, Alan Hullings, the janitor at the Trenton Junction Public School, was attacked by a tramp who was attempting to rob him. The attack was foiled, however, by Hulling's dog—a Collie—who heard the scuffle and ran to his master's defense. The dog's attack was so fierce that the tramp ran away.[114]

Pietro Sanegari was not as lucky. The 30-year-old was lying near death in McKinley Hospital in Trenton after being involved in an "altercation and stabbing affray in one of the shanties" in the Trenton

---

[112] Trenton Times, September 22, 1890.

[113] Trenton Times, May 2, 1904. In a strange and unexplained twist, the following day, May 3, 1904, an article rain in the Trenton Times that stated "William Simpkins, of Trenton Junction, was arrested [May 2nd] by Constable Howell on a charge of assault and battery with intent to kill, preferred by Charles Hunt, also of Trenton Junction. He was held for the grand jury under $200 bail by 'Squire Mills." No further explanation or articles can be found!

[114] Trenton Times, March 9, 1905.

Junction Railroad Camp. He had been attacked by Luigi Sabastine, another laborer living in the camp, who escaped.[115]

While the aforementioned assaults were bad, there were some that were so heinous that it placed the entire village of Trenton Junction in an uproar. They were the cases that everyone knew about and that everyone talked about.

Louella Marshall

While the tragic story of Louella Marshall did not occur in Trenton Junction, it did, however, occur nearby and was of such magnitude that it was most assuredly on the minds and tongues of the local residents.

Thirty-three-year-old Louella B. Marshall lived on one of the farms along the old Pennington Road, not far from the Odd Fellows' Home. In the early evening hours of December 3, 1912, she was walking along Pennington Road, returning home from a shopping trip in Trenton. Suddenly, she was attacked, "struck down from behind with a heavy bludgeon, which fractured her skull. Another blow of the same weapon broke the bones of her jaw. The murderous assailant then dragged his unresisting victim into a field back of the roadway fence. This fence is constructed of barbed wire, and the man dragged his victim over the barbs, ripping off her clothing and tearing long gashes in her flesh. Before he had completed his fiendish work he had torn the young woman's clothing to ribbons."

Possibly startled by the approach of another pedestrian, the assailant fled. Agnes Eggert, a neighbor of Louella's, happened to be walking along the same roadway. She saw a man "…hurrying out of the wooded field where the assault took place," but it was so dark that she was unable to identify the person. Suddenly, Agnes heard groans coming from the field and she found Louella, lying in the grass, beaten, broken and bleeding. Another neighbor, Wallace Lanning, also happened to see a man running across the field. An

---

[115] Asbury Park Press, July 5, 1910.

ambulance was called and Louella was rushed to Mercer Hospital. Examination by doctors there found that she had suffered a fractured skull, broken nose and the loss of several teeth. She was in and out of consciousness and in critical condition. When conscious, she was irrational and delirious.

Because of her delirium, the police were unable to get any clues as to her assailant's identity or description, first saying, "...he was a negro and next declaring [he] was a white man." Wallace Lanning believed he saw an African-American man running across the field; Agnes Eggert could not tell the man's race. Plaster casts were taken of footprints that indicated shoes about 7 ½ in size.

A $250 reward was immediately posted by Louella's uncle, Lewis A. Marshall, a retired storekeeper from Trenton, for the capture of her assailant. Her employers added $500 and the Mercer County Board of Chosen Freeholders also offered $500.

Prosecutor Crossley and Detective Clancy of the Trenton Police Department formed "a posse of police and citizens" and searched the surrounding countryside in an attempt to find her assailant. After a fruitless thirty-six hour search, Sheriff Maddon of Mercer County brought in bloodhounds. [116]

The bloodhounds tracked down Edward Chapman, a "powerfully built" 41-year-old African-American man living in a nearby "negro settlement." "Only the intervention of the more cool headed members of the posse prevented the searchers from taking matters into their own hands. Talk of lynching...[had] been heard on all sides as the search [had] progressed." Investigation by police quickly exonerated Chapman of the brutal crime.

A week after the brutal attack, Louella Marshall succumbed to her wounds and the "John Doe" warrant issued for her assailant was immediately changed from "atrocious assault" to "murder." Two

---

[116] In January 1913, Assemblyman Holcombe of Hunterdon County introduced a bill in the State Assembly requiring "sheriffs in the several counties of the state to keep bloodhounds for the detection of criminals. When the Marshall crime occurred Sheriff Maddon...had to send to Hoboken to get dogs to track the criminal. (Asbury Park Press, January 16, 1913).

days later, New Jersey's Acting Governor John Dyneley Prince issued a proclamation adding $1,000 to the reward. Although her funeral was private, "...a great crowd, consisting mostly of women and girls, surrounded the house [of her Uncle] while the services were being held." She was buried in Riverview Cemetery alongside the grave of her mother, Emily, who had died five years earlier. That same day, the Coroner began his inquest.

The following night, the police arrested William Mansfield in connection with Louella's murder. "Mansfield, who is white and about 30 years old, was stop[ed] near the scene of the assault. He has scratches on his hand and the police say his shoes correspond with the footprints at the scene of the attack." However, just as in the case of Edward Chapman, further investigation cleared him of any connection with the crime. The coroner's jury, meanwhile, finished their investigation but was unable to uncover any clues as to the identity of the attacker. The jury could only render a verdict that the young woman's death was caused by an assault committed on her by some persons unknown to the jury.

The coroner's jury did, however, make a very important recommendation: that the state should establish a "state constabulary for the protection of outlying districts." This, added to the outcry of the farmers and members of the grange, eventually led to the creation of the New Jersey State Police in March 1921.[117]

William Alzenholfer was a German immigrant working as a farm hand on a dairy farm on the outskirts of Trenton. Shortly before New Years' Eve, Alzenholfer, a morphine addict found himself under the care of Nurse Ida Capen and Doctor Joseph Denelsbeck. He appeared obsessed with the Marshall case and this raised a red flag with his nurse.

> The first intimation that Atzenhafer was connected to the crime came to Miss Capen, whose suspicions were aroused by the man's eagerness to obtain information from

---

[117] The Scranton Republican (Scranton, Pennsylvania), December 18, 1912.

newspapers regarding Miss Marshall's condition before her death and the movements of police afterward. Miss Capen communicated her suspicions to Dr. Denelsbeck...Dr. Denelsbeck interviewed Atzenhafer and became convinced that he was Miss Marshall's assailant. He caused the suspect to come to Trenton and housed him in a hotel. Then the physician informed the police and a confession was readily obtained. Altzenhafer told Prosecutor William J. Crossley, of Mercer County, that he attacked Miss Marshall, but declared he mistook her for another person and that he did not intend to kill her. When questioned as to whom he thought he was attacking, [he] said that he had no reason to attack anyone. Further questioning brought from Atzenhafer the fact that the attack was made with the two and a half foot length of pipe found by the side of Miss Marshall's unconscious form the night of the crime. [He] said he got the pipe from the rear of the two houses in course of construction near the scene of the crime. He added that after he struck Miss Marshall he dragged her body across the road, through a barbed wire fence and left her unconscious in the field upon the approach of two men.[118]

City detectives faced great disappointment as they quickly came to realize that William Atzenholfer was "suffering from hallucinations and that owing to the fact that his mind has been weakened by morphine... he is not fully responsible for his statements." Furthermore, the police determined that he was "not in the vicinity of the crime" when the assault occurred. Detectives believed that his arrest shortly after the crime and the fact that he was "reading frequently of the murder have so worked upon the farmhand's mind that he believed himself to be the guilty man and confessed. It is pointed out that a crime of this character usually brings forward many cranks, who claim to have had something to do with it or else to be able to solve it." Although he

---

[118] The Bristol Daily Courier (Bristol, Pennsylvania), December 30, 1912.

was still held without bail and charged with murder, three years later newspapers still declared the crime unsolved.[119]

Catherine Phaler

With Louella Marshall's horrible murder very fresh in everyone's mind, another violent assault occurred. But this time, it was much closer to home, as Catherine Phaler was a local Trenton Junction girl and just 14 years old.

Catherine Phaler was born in 1899, the daughter of a well-to-do farmer who lived in Trenton Junction on the Picturesque Poultry Farm along the Asylum Road. A Roman Catholic, Catherine had travelled into Trenton to arrange for her Confirmation at a Catholic church in town the following Sunday. It was about 8:30 in the evening when she left for home, accompanied by the daughter of Christopher Buggy, the coachman at the State Hospital (Yes that really was his name and occupation). When they reached the entrance to the Asylum grounds,

---

[119] Wilkes-Barre Times Leader, the Evening News (Wilkes-Barre, Pennsylvania), Asbury Park Press, Altoona Tribune (Altoona, Pennsylvania), December 4, 1912; Altoona Tribune (Altoona, Pennsylvania), Mount Carmel Item (Mount Carmel, Pennsylvania), Asbury Park Press, The York Daily (York, Pennsylvania), The Scranton Republican (Scranton, Pennsylvania), Williamsport Sun-Gazette (Williamsport, Pennsylvania), Harrisburg Telegraph, December 5, 1912; Asbury Park Press, December 6, 1912; Reading Times (Reading, Pennsylvania), December 7, 1912; Lebanon Daily News (Lebanon, Pennsylvania) December 10, 1912; The Scranton Republican (Scranton, Pennsylvania), Altoona Tribune (Altoona, Pennsylvania), The Wilkes-Barre Record (Wilkes-Barre, Pennsylvania), December 11, 1912; Harrisburg Daily Independent, December 12, 1912; The Gettysburg Times (Gettysburg, Pennsylvania), Trenton Evening Times, December 13, 1912; Asbury Park Press, December 14, 1912; Williamsport Sun-Gazette (Williamsport, Pennsylvania), December 16, 1912; The Scranton Republican (Scranton, Pennsylvania), December 18, 1912; The San Francisco Call, December 29, 1912; The Wilkes-Barre Record (Wilkes-Barre, Pennsylvania), The Bristol Daily Courier (Bristol, Pennsylvania), Asbury Park Press, December 30, 1912; Asbury Park Press, December 31, 1912; Asbury Park Press, March 14, 1913; Trenton Evening Times, March 15, 1929.

"they alighted from the [trolley] car" and Catherine continued to walk up the lonely, dark road alone.

Catherine was just about a quarter of a mile from her home when she was suddenly attacked by a man who sprang at her from behind a tree. She struggled with the man, "...but he threw her to the ground and dragged her into the bushes, breaking three fingers on her right hand in the struggle to hold her. She was still fighting him when the sound of an approaching wagon frightened him off." At that point, Catherine fainted. Unfortunately, the driver of the wagon did not notice her and she lay, unconscious, on the side of the road for several hours.

Jacob Pfeister, a telegrapher for the railroad, was at his key in the railroad tower office when he heard groans outside. He left his post to investigate and found Catherine dazed and barely conscious on the side of the road, her clothes torn and her body was cut and badly bruised. He recognized her and took her to the home of Glen Bellis, the manager of the Picturesque Poultry Farm.

It was dark and Catherine did not get a look at the person who attacked her from behind. Incredibly, the police did not believe her story and claimed that they were unable to find any evidence of an assault having been attempted! They were "inclined to believe [Catherine had] imagined much of what she said had happened to her." Eventually, they came to their senses and detectives uncovered a suspect—Sherman Cooper, a young motorman working on the trolley line.

The police went to Cooper's home in Trenton to confront him and he made a full confession. He was held under a minor charge on just $200 bail.[120]

---

[120] The Picturesque Poultry Farm & Hatchery was located opposite the Trenton Country Club where Palmer Lane and the Versailles Apartments are currently located. It was established in 1882 and was known internationally for its breeding of quality March 15, 1913.birds. It was owned by the Breese family of Trenton.

New York Times, March 15, 1913.The Evening World (New York), Asbury Park Press, March 14, 1913; New York Times, Asbury Park Press, Evening Report (Lebanon, Pennsylvania), Trenton Evening Times, March 15, 1913.

Mrs. Mary Elizabeth Van Lieu

As horrible as the crimes and attacks described above were, the most heinous crime committed within the boundaries of Trenton Junction has to be the murder of Mrs. Mary Van Lieu.

George and Mary Elizabeth Van Lieu, along with their two-year-old son, William, were a "much respected negro family" living on the outskirts of Trenton Junction, about a mile north of the crossroads. "George was an industrious man," and he made a good living as a farm hand working for various farmers around Trenton Junction. About four o'clock in the afternoon of Saturday, November 17, 1900, George Van Lieu left their home to go into Trenton, where he would play his violin and banjo "...in the saloons and in this way add to the small earnings of the week." While making his way to town, Van Lieu ran into Robert Henson. They knew each other; in fact Henson had been a frequent visitor to the Van Lieu homestead and little William "...had grown to love him so that he called him 'Bob'. Henson also loved the child." After a brief chat, each went their own way.

When George returned home later that evening, he arrived to find his home had been destroyed by a terrible fire. When he realized his wife and son were nowhere to be seen, he assumed they had taken refuge at a neighbor's house. He went knocking door to door but could not find his family. Worried, he contacted the Mercer County authorities. Prosecutor Crossley and three detectives arrived at the scene and a search ensued. About an hour after rummaging through the burned remnants of what was once his home, "the charred remains of the mother and baby were found in the cellar, where they had fallen with the collapse of the building."

The bodies were so badly burned that the Coroner was not able to determine if they had been mutilated prior to death, "but the presence of an axe in the cellar near the bodies affords a clue to the way the murder was committed. The axe, when Van Lieu left home, was outside in a shed near the spot where a pool of blood was found."

George Van Lieu told police that he had run into Robert Henson while on his way into Trenton. Neighbors also reported seeing Henson in the area. Police Captain Hartman decided to track him down.

Henson's actions were suspicious. After being seen going in the direction of the Van Lieu house, he "...was next seen that night about midnight at the home of a negress named Ann Smith, who lives a mile or two above where the van Lieu house stood...The next day he wandered over to Pennington, then returned to Ann Smith's Sunday afternoon only to walk over to Washington's Crossing in the evening...After following Henson to Ann Smith's and to Pennington they were sure he was the man, so they went to Andrew Williamson's at Washington Crossing, Sunday night, and managed to arrest Henson after considerable trouble."

Captain Harman determined that after meeting George Van Lieu Saturday afternoon, Henson continued on to the Van Lieu house where he found Mary Elizabeth and her son alone. "He entered the house and is supposed to have made an indecent proposal to the woman, who resented it."

Angered by the rebuff, Henson attacked the woman. She escaped to the yard and Henson followed after her. He caught up with her near a water pump and attacked her, killing her with an axe from a nearby woodpile. Then, in an attempt to cover up the crime, he dragged her body into the house and set fire to it.

Henson suddenly remembered little William Van Lieu who was sleeping upstairs. Not wanting to kill the baby, he went upstairs and carried him, "blanket and all, out of the house, across a newly ploughed field and placed him alongside the fence. The child awoke and, recognizing Henson gave a cry. Henson now feared that the child would tell of seeing him there that night and so he was compelled to kill the child which it is believed he did by stabbing him with his pocket knife. Then, he carried the baby back up to the house and laid him beside his dead mother. The house was then fired and Henson sneaked away through the back roads to Ann Smith's where he spent the night."

This was not Robert Henson's first arrest. He confessed on cross-examination at his trial that he had been convicted of assault and battery and atrocious assault and battery. Thirteen years prior, in November 1887, he was arrested and charged with the mutilation-murder of Ella

Quinn, "a white woman [from Trenton] who was his mistress, but sufficient evidence was not obtained to hold him." Just weeks before the Van Lieu murder, Henson had been released from jail after serving a sentence for larceny.

Robert Henson went to trial in February 1901 in the Mercer County Court and was found guilty of *triple* homicide—Mary Elizabeth Van Lieu, it was discovered, was expecting her second child—and he was sentenced to hang on April 25th. His attorneys, Beasley and Walker, immediately took the case to the Court of Errors and Appeals "... claiming that there were several errors in the trial of the case in the lower court and asking for a new trial. The higher court took until November [1901] to render a decision and then it sustained the rulings of Justice Gummere in the lower court," eight justices to six. [121] He was re-sentenced on December 6th, and December 27, 1901, was named as the new date for his execution. The Court of Pardons refused to commute Henson's death sentence.

While he was awaiting execution, Henson "gave frequent exhibitions of his temper, having assaulted his keepers on different occasions. During the past month it has been necessary to chain him to the floor of his cell." Then, at 11:08 in the morning of December 27th, Robert Henson was taken from his cell in the Mercer County Jail and led to the scaffold.

"Accompanied by Father Fox and Father Callahan, Henseon walked steadily up the scaffold steps with his eyes always fixed on the crucifix, held before him by Father Fox...Sheriff Atchley asked, 'Robert is there anything you have to say before the sentence of the law is passed upon you?' Without taking his eyes from the crucifix, Hensen replied in a husky voice, 'Nothing; good-bye all.'" The sheriff then pulled the black cap over the face of the unfortunate man and a moment later shoved the lever that opened the trap doors." It was 11:11 a.m.

---

[121] The New Jersey State Constitution of 1844 provided for two avenues of appeal—the Court of Errors and Appeals and the Court of Pardons. This was not changed until the late 1940s when the State Constitution was re-written and the judicial branch was revamped to the system that we have today.

The hanging took place in the yard of the Mercer Jail on Broad and Market Streets in Trenton, a dozen feet from the rear entrance. As would be expected with a case of this notoriety, a large crowd had gathered at the time of the execution. In the crowd were many children from the local schools. After the hanging, the local police were permitted to view Henson's body. "The gates were wide, so that when they were opened to admit the police, the children had a full view of the murderer" hanging from the scaffold.

Henson's body was cut down and turned over to undertaker Harry Ashmore, who buried him in the pauper's plot in Riverview Cemetery.[122]

---

[122] The Pittsburg Daily Headlight (Pittsburg, Kansas),the Wilkes-Barre Record (Wilkes-Barre, Pennsylvania), The Times (Philadelphia), The Charlotte news (Charlotte, North Carolina), November 19, 1900; The Raleigh Times (Raleigh, North Carolina), The Portsmouth Herald (Portsmouth, New Hampshire), The Morning News (Wilmington, Delaware), New-York Tribune, The Times (Philadelphia, Pennsylvania), November 20, 1900; Lebanon Courier and Semi-Weekly Report (Lebanon, Pennsylvania), November 21, 1900; The Citizen (Berea, Kentucky), November 23, 1900; The Times (Philadelphia, Pennsylvania), November 23, 1900; The Times (Philadelphia), January 19, 1901; New York Times, December 7, 1901; The Times (Philadelphia), December 19, 1901; The Times (Philadelphia), December 25, 1901; Vicksburg Evening Post (Vicksburg, Mississippi), The Charlotte News (Charlotte, North Carolina), December 26, 1901; The Charlotte News (Charlotte, North Carolina, Fort Wayne Daily News (Fort Wayne, Indiana), Trenton Times, December 27, 1901; The Atlanta Constitution (Atlanta, Georgia), The Daily Chronicle (De Kalb, Illinois), The Charlotte Observer (Charlotte, North Carolina) December 28, 1901.

CHAPTER 12

THE BLAST THAT SHOOK TRENTON JUNCTION

I T STARTED OUT AS a quiet Friday night in late September, 1932. Ewing Township Recorder John Boscarell[123] was in his home on Grand Avenue, "two doors away from the main intersection." Having finished dinner, he made his way upstairs to check on his three-year-old son, Jack, who was sleeping. Something told him to move his son's crib into the middle of the room, away from the window. He then went downstairs, and, leaving his mother-in-law Mary Sauber in the front room and his wife Pauline sitting in the dining room listening to the radio, Recorder Boscarell made his way to the Ewing Township Police Headquarters, where he was a magistrate.

Shortly before nine o'clock that evening, Mrs. Boscarell smelled acrid fumes. Thinking the odor could be from burning insulation on electric wires or a short-circuited fuse, she left the dining room to go upstairs to investigate. No sooner had she reached the top step when the bomb exploded.

"After the deafening roar and the sound of splintering wood and

---

[123] Recorder is a judicial title, below that of a Justice of the Peace. A Recorder's Court usually just hears misdemeanors, traffic violations and petty criminal offenses.

the foundation stones toppling into the cellar, [Mrs. Boscarell and Mrs. Sauber] called to one another, hurried to the nursery to pick up the child and then went outside." They then made their way to the Sauber home on Central Avenue, about two blocks away. While no one was injured, they were quite understandably very shaken.

The explosion was felt all through Trenton Junction and as far away as the city of Trenton. The neighbors were shaken from their beds. Pauline Boscarell narrowly escaped death—had she not gone upstairs to investigate the acrid odor, she would have been sitting in the room of the house most severely damaged by the explosion. Her husband's action of moving the crib most likely saved his son's life since "part of the flooring where it originally stood was ripped away by the explosion."

Ewing Township Police Officer Clarence E. Morris led the investigation, with the assistance of New Jersey State Police Sergeant John Wallace and County Detective Edward Leadem. It was quickly learned that a bomb was placed under a bay window of the dining room.[124] "The dynamite or other powerful explosive left a gaping hole in the foundation at a rear corner of the [house] and tore away considerable woodwork. Ten windows on that side of the house were shattered." Florence Winkel, who lived across the street from the Boscarells, said that the explosion "shook her home violently. When she looked out, she saw a heavy cloud of smoke arising from the side of the opposite home and heard a clatter of breaking glass. However, she did not observe anyone in the vicinity nor see any autos leaving the scene."

It would have been very easy for the person who planted the explosives "to have had a car waiting just around the corner, where the highway gives swift access to Scotch Road or the River Road or flight in the direction of Mercer Airport by following Grand Avenue

---

[124] According to the September 26, 1932 edition of the Trenton Evening Times, "had the dynamite been placed in a metal container, or had some high explosive been placed in the form of a bomb, then the explosion would have been sufficiently great to wreck the house and possibly kill all the occupants."

out of West Trenton. [Boscarell's] house is only two doors away from the main intersection of the community."

Initially, some of the neighbors suggested to police that a "band of gypsies" was responsible for the explosion, two of whom had been arrested just a few days earlier for fighting in another part of the township.[125] Others thought that someone was jealous of John Boscarell. After all, he had "...risen rapidly in public life being active politically in the township where he served as Township Committeeman for a time prior to his appointment to the present position" of Recorder. The police dismissed these theories and had one of their own.

Officer Morris remembered that 21-year-old Charlie Ratico, a Trenton Junction resident, had recently been sentenced to thirty days in the workhouse as a result of a "fistic encounter" [fist-fight] he had with John Boscarell. He had been released the Monday prior to the explosion and allegedly threatened that "he would get Boscarell." That was enough for Morris to arrest Ratico later Friday night on suspicion. Also arrested was Ratico's best friend, 20-year-old Tony Sebasto. They were held overnight in the county jail, protesting their innocence.[126]

The police had no clues and they would soon have to release their suspects. But Officer Morris had an idea. Early Saturday morning, Officer Morris took Tony Sebastio back to the Boscarell house. He led him up to the nursery where three-year-old Jack had been sleeping at the time of the blast and proceeded to question him. "Morris kept the prisoner in the room all day, maintaining a rapid fire of questions.

---

[125] It was not uncommon for bands of gypsies to pass through the area. In 1902, a band of eight or nine gypsies passed through Trenton Junction. They had two dancing bears, a monkey and two wagons. (Trenton Times, January 28, 1902).

[126] Charles Ratico was arrested on August 25, 1932, on a charge of disorderly conduct, remanded to the county jail for one day, and then taken away by a township officer to spend 30 days in the county workhouse. He was released on September 19, 1932. Anthony Sebasto had been arrested in June 1931 for violation of a township ordinance and served ten days in the county jail. (Trenton Evening Times, September 26, 1932).

Sebasto maintained that he was innocent until shortly after 7 o'clock [that] night. Morris had given him a brief respite from the quizzing. Suddenly, he began to press the suspect for an account of his actions Friday night" and Sebasto cracked. "'I'll tell you all I know and get it over with. Charlie Ratico and I did it!'"

According to Sebasto's statement, he met up with Charlie Ratico Friday night and Charlie asked him to help him with a plan to "scare" Boscarell. Just before 9 o'clock that evening, the two of them walked to the side of Boscarell's house. "Ratico had seven sticks of dynamite...and Ratico told him that he planned to detonate the explosives alongside the [house]. Sebasto protested because he feared someone might be injured, but Ratico assured him that the explosion would 'just knock a hole in the wall.'" Besides, they saw Boscarell's car diving away earlier in the evening so they assumed, even though there were lights on in the house, that no one was home.

Sebasto continued:

> ...accusing Ratico of digging a hole near the foundation and lighting the fuse. Then, both left, going to Ratico's home near the railroad camp. They had been in the house only a few minutes...when the dynamite let go with a concussion that shook West Trenton. A few minutes later the youths walked to the center of West Trenton. Ratico remained at the principal corner while Sebasto says he walked to a point in front of the house to see what damage had been caused.[127]

As soon as Officer Morris obtained Sebasto's signature on his statement, he, along with State Police Detective Wallace and Ewing Police Chief Harry Prince returned to the county jail where they confronted Charlie Ratico. Ratico was taken to the State Police Training School at Wilburtha where his confession was obtained.

In his statement Ratico told the police that,

---

[127] The newspaper refers to West Trenton instead of Trenton Junction because Trenton Junction had officially changed its name to West Trenton only that previous June.

"...the dynamite which was used had been in his possession since early in the summer when he found it along the canal bank near Wilburtha. His motive for setting it off, he declared, was to obtain revenge for the Workhouse term which he had received. He said he planned the bombing while a prisoner at the Workhouse, and upon his release, broached the plan with Sebasto and asked him for his aid. Ratico said that he once worked in a quarry and in that manner became familiar with the handling of the explosive. Last Thursday, he added, he obtained the dynamite from a spot where he had buried it and concealed it near the Boscarell home. On Friday night...he and Sebasto, after having several drinks of liquor, procured the explosive and walked to Boscarell's home. They got a shovel from a shed in an adjoining yard, dug a hole along the foundation and placed the powder. After lighting the fuse...they returned to his home and had a few more drinks.[128]

In the morning of September 27, 1932, the two Trenton Junction men appeared before Judge Schroth in Mercer Court and Mercer County Prosecutor Erwin Marshall appeared to handle the cases personally. Charles Ratico and Anthony Sebasto both pleaded guilty, agreed to forego indictment by the Grand Jury and to stay in jail pending sentencing and then "...signed waivers to avoid a 42-hour delay required by law under normal circumstances."

Sentencing was carried out after an extended conference between Prosecutor Marshall and Judge Schroth in chambers. Back on the bench, Judge Schroth stated, "'this is a very grave offense. You just missed causing the death of three persons, two women and a small child. It was an act of the most dangerous and dastardly character. The protection of the public from outrages of this kind requires a severe penalty.'" Charles Ratico was then sentenced to 12 to 15 years and Anthony Sebasto was sentenced to 10 to 12 years. "Less than 90 hours

---

[128] Trenton Sunday Times Advertiser, September 23, 1932. It was the "burning fuse" that Pauline Boscarell thought she smelled that caused her to leave the room to investigate, thereby most likely saving her from injury or death.

had elapsed between the crime and the arrival of the defendants at the prison." But the story does not end here!

On the evening of September 26th, Louis Garzio, the 44-year-old next door neighbor of John Boscarell, was arrested and "committed to jail in default of bail." The police had learned from Charles Ratico that he had confided his plan to detonate the dynamite to Garzio. "Garzio warned him against the action, however Garzio failed to report to police before or after the crime occurred and his arrest followed."

Initially Garzio was released on bail. However, investigators received additional information "…which sent officers scurrying to his home…with a warrant." Garzio was not at home, however the next morning he, accompanied by his attorney, surrendered to Prosecutor Marshall.

Judge Schroth held Louis Garzio on $15,000 bail as a principal in the bombing case. His lawyer, Meyer M. Semel of Newark, objected strenuously, saying that it was too high. "Don't you think it is unreasonable that this man, who lives next door to Mr. Boscarell, should have anything to do with a plot that would endanger his own family of a wife and eight children?" Prosecutor Marshall claimed he had evidence showing that Garzio was actually the man "who engineered the job."

Prosecutor Marshall had learned that the fist fight between Charles Ratico and John Boscarell that led to Ratico spending a month in the workhouse—and the subsequent "grudge" that led to him planting the bomb—came about because of a young girl. Ratico "displayed great affection" for a girl "who was wronged by another youth." Ratico became angry with Boscarell when he was retained as counsel by that "youth" in a civil suit filed by the girl's family. It was soon learned that "…Garzio was deeply interested in a civil suit, the same one cited by Ratico…in which Boscarell appeared as counsel for the opposition. Prosecutor Marshall said the civil suit concerned a daughter of Garzio."

The story had come full circle. Regardless, Louis Garzio was a very well-liked resident of Trenton Junction. To help with his bail, "a total of ten persons pledged their properties…pooling their assets to supply $24,000 security for his appearance in court....Approximately a dozen properties were involved, being located in Trenton, Hamilton Township, and Pennington...." Initially, the bail was set at $15,000 but Judge Schroth consented to lowering it to $12,000. However, because Garzio's supporters were giving property in lieu of cash for the bail, *double* the amount was required.[129]

---

[129] The Evening Times (Sayre, Pennsylvania), The Brooklyn Daily Eagle, Lincoln Evening Journal (Lincoln, Nebraska), Middletown Times Herald (Middletown, New York), Asbury Park Press, Trenton Evening Times, September 24, 1932; Trenton Sunday Times Advertiser, September 25, 1932; Trenton Evening Times, September 26, 1932; Trenton Evening Times, September 27, 1932; Asbury Park Press, Trenton Evening Times, September 28, 1932; Philadelphia Inquirer, September 29, 1932; Trenton Evening Times, September 30, 1932.

CHAPTER 13

THE MAD SCIENTIST OF TRENTON JUNCTION

TRENTON JUNCTION WAS NOT immune from the hazards of disease. Medicine in the late nineteenth and early twentieth centuries pales in comparison to modern medicine. Many vaccines that we have today simply did not exist, and those that did were not always effective. Penicillin and other antibiotics were unheard of, so that something as simple as stepping on a tack could be life threatening. For example, eighteen-year-old Mary Barden of Augusta, Georgia, was visiting her aunt in Trenton Junction in the autumn months of 1904. She was "a beautiful girl...considered a belle in the social circles of Augusta." One morning, while walking across her bedroom, she stepped on a tack. Confined to the hospital for several months and with no tetanus vaccine available (it was not discovered until 1924), doctors decided that it was necessary to amputate her leg in order to save her life.[130]

In 1894, Thomas Sewell, an African-American farm laborer in Trenton Junction was found to be suffering from *varioloid,* a mild form of smallpox suffered by those who had already had the disease. He was confined in the outbuilding of a farm until Overseer B.C. Baldwin of

---

[130] The Scranton Republican (Scranton, Pennsylvania), January 26, 1905.

the Board of Health moved him to a small house owned by Doctor Hough in the woods nearby. "Food and proper attention will be given him here by the Township Committee and a close watch will be kept to prevent him from communicating with anyone in order to insure against the spread of the dreaded disease."[131]

In 1905, there was a case of smallpox in the railroad camp. One of the Italian laborers contracted the disease in Philadelphia and brought it back with him to Trenton Junction. The barracks were fumigated and other precautions were taken to prevent the spread of the disease. The patient was taken to the Municipal Hospital in Hamilton Township.

Doctor E.B. Allen reported that there was no indication of any spread of smallpox in Trenton Junction. He declared that the laborers who were associated with the victim were being kept away from the public and those "Italians who have been about the station have no connection with the gang." Disaster had been averted.[132]

There is no record of anyone in Trenton Junction dying from smallpox and the authorities were able to contain the two known outbreaks. They were also quick to contain an outbreak of scarlet fever. In May 1903, the school in Trenton Junction was closed indefinitely "… on account of scarlet fever which prevailed among the scholars. It was said that the fever started with a little girl in an [African-American] family named Green who live on the Harbourton Road." Within days it had spread to the families of John Callahan, Eugene Starr, and Theodore Ivins. Fortunately, no one died.[133]

Trenton Junction did not have its own hospital. If a patient's needs were beyond what could be treated by a doctor's house call, the patient would need to be transported to one of the three Trenton hospitals: Mercer, St. Francis, and the William McKinley Memorial Hospital,

---

[131] Trenton Times, March 22, 1894.

[132] Trenton Times, December 20 & 23, 1905.

[133] Trenton Times, May 18, 1903.

later called Helene Fuld. The "State Hospital" on what is now called Sullivan Way was not a medical hospital but rather one for psychiatric care.

Technically, the New Jersey State Psychiatric Hospital—known in the late nineteenth and early twentieth centuries as "The State Lunatic Asylum"—was not in Trenton Junction; rather it was in the Brookville section of Ewing (an area later annexed by the City of Trenton). Because it lies right on the border, it was often pushed across that border by the newspapers.

Established in 1844 by philanthropist and mental health advocate Dorothea Dix, the first public mental hospital in the state of New Jersey officially opened on May 15, 1848, for the treatment of the mentally ill. For many, the Asylum was seen as a scary place. Not least of all because of one of the doctors. Doctor Henry Cotton could be considered a genuine mad scientist. And he worked just down the road from Trenton Junction.

"Few experiments in the field of psychology were more horrifying that those conducted by Doctor Henry Cotton in the Trenton State Hospital…In many cases, he all but butchered his patients in an effort to heal their minds." Undeniably, Doctor Cotton was a well-educated scientist. He had studied under Doctor Emil Kraepelin, Doctor Adolf Meyer and Doctor Alois Alzheimer. These men were the "pillars in the field of psychiatry in the early 1900s. Doctor Meyer…observed that patients with very high fevers could suffer hallucinations. From this, he hypothesized that infections might be the root cause of behavioral abnormalities." Doctor Cotton latched on to that theory and ran with it.

In 1906, Doctor Cotton became the medical director of the Trenton State Hospital where he implemented the practice of "surgical bacteriology." The theory was that if an infection of certain body parts (called "focal sepsis") caused insanity, removing that body part would cure the patient. "Cotton would begin by pulling patient's teeth. If the patient failed to show improvement, he might remove the tonsils next. If again there was no improvement, he would move to steadily more major surgeries, including removing—partially or in total—testicles, ovaries, gall bladders, stomachs, and spleens. [He] was especially interested in how suspected colon infections would impact psychological health, and he often removed whole sections of people's intestines."

While Doctor Cotton claimed he had an 85 percent success rate—which garnered him high praise from his fellow scientists—the reality was just the opposite. Many of the patients "...were left toothless and suffered unnecessary surgeries in pursuit of a cure that did not exist. Doctor Cotton, who was not a trained surgeon, performed abdominal surgeries in the age before penicillin. Death rates from the needless procedures were as high as 45 percent. Less extreme forms of surgical bacteriology were performed in Trenton State Hospital until the 1950s."

Patients and their families as well as former employees began to complain and an investigation was begun. During the investigation, Doctor Cotton "...apparently suffered a nervous breakdown, which he treated by pulling several teeth. He pronounced himself cured." He finally retired in 1930 and was appointed medical director emeritus. He died three years later of a heart attack.[134]

Imagine if you found yourself trapped in that hospital—as a sane person committed there against your will. That actually happened in 1924. A story was reported in the Reno, Nevada *Reno Gazette-Journal* and *The Capital Times* of Madison, Wisconsin about Mrs. Frank W. French. She was the estranged young wife of a Newark, New Jersey broker. In January 1924, she was in seclusion in New York City after filing a suit for $1,000,000 against three people—including her mother, Helen Darling—"in connection with charges that they had conspired to keep her in a sanitarium at Trenton Junction" against her will. Mrs. French was able to escape from the asylum "by climbing from a window down an improvised rope of twisted bed clothing."[135]

Twenty-seven-year-old Samuel Giron of Trenton Junction was a patient at the asylum as well, but in 1922 he was pronounced "cured

[134] http://www.oddlyhistorical.com/2014/06/10/infectious-insanity-dr-henry-cotton-practice-surgical-bacteriology/.

[135] The Capital Times (Madison, Wisconsin), January 2, 1924; Reno Gazette-Journal, (Nevada). January 19, 1924.

of insanity" and released. As can be imagined, he was terrified of the prospect of ever going back to the hospital of horrors. He was so scared that on the night of August 18, 1922, he dreamed that the hospital guards were trying to capture him and take him back. While still asleep and dreaming, Giron jumped from his bed and made his way onto his roof. He then "leaped into the flue, falling to a point near the ground. He became [stuck] and members of the family sent word to the Trenton Fire Department. After trying unsuccessfully to pull the man out with ropes, the firemen had to cut a hole in the wall. Giron was nearly suffocated, but was revived."[136]

—⚏—

Disease and mental illness were not the only medical challenges facing Trenton Junction. In rural communities, farm related injuries were not uncommon. Some even made it into the newspapers. For example, in 1902, Gus Spencer, a farm hand, fell from a load of hay. He was badly bruised and one leg was lacerated. He was rushed to McKinley Hospital where Doctor Brown attended to his injuries.[137]

John Cook was a laborer working on John Thackeray's farm. While helping thresh wheat one day, he "hit his head against one of the fly-wheels on the machine, and but for the quickness of the other helpers, would have been killed." He was knocked unconscious. Cook suffered a two inch cut on his scalp and another cut over his eye. He was treated on the farm by Dr. E.B. Allen and eventually recovered.[138]

The summer of 1907 was a busy time for Dr. Allen. Just two months before John Cook's injury, Charles Lawrence, the Trenton Junction Postmaster, was in need of his services. Mr. Lawrence was cutting bananas from a stalk when his knife slipped "…and penetrated

---

[136] Los Angeles Times, August 19, 1922; The Post-Crescent (Appleton, Wisconsin). August 19, 1922; New York Times, August 19, 1922; The Bremen Enquirer (Bremen, Indiana), September 21, 1922.
[137] Trenton Evening Times, September 10, 1902.
[138] Trenton Evening Times, September 18, 1907.

the flesh just below the stomach." Remarkably, it was not a serious injury.[139]

Constable Joseph Wagner of the Ewing Township Police Department was not so lucky. He was badly hurt while riding the Trenton Junction trolley. When attempting to step from the trolley car, he was jolted to one side "and came in violent contact with the controller" mechanism. A blood vessel burst in his stomach and his condition was serious.[140]

Trolleys could be hazardous, as Joseph Wagner learned. Mrs. Francis Lanning learned that lesson, as well. While riding the trolley from Trenton Junction into the city, a truck made a sharp turn near the trolley tracks. A pipe projecting from the rear of a truck crashed through the window by her seat and fractured her skull, leaving her in critical condition at McKinley Hospital. The driver of the truck, C.B. Hirst, was arrested and held in the county jail without bail.[141]

Twenty-year-old Angelo DeFranze was working on the construction of a building in Trenton Junction when he was struck by a beam that had swung from a derrick. He was rushed to Mercer Hospital with severe contusions of the back.[142]

Before the advent of automobiles, the common mode of transportation was horse and wagon. Like cars, this form of transportation could be quite dangerous. William B. Fort was a Trenton Junction resident who worked as a milkman. One morning

---

[139] Trenton Evening Times, July 3, 1907.
[140] Trenton Evening Times, January 22, 1907.
[141] Asbury Park Press, July 18, 1922.
[142] Trenton Evening Times, July 13, 1910.

in January 1896, he was making a delivery on Spring Street when the horse attached to his milk wagon started to run away. Fort grabbed the handles on both sides of the door and, with great effort managed to swing back into the wagon. He took hold of the reins and was able to stop the horse. "The violent effort, however, proved too much for him and he strained both his limbs from the knee downwards." His brother Edward took him home and was able to nurse him back to health.[143]

Joseph Atchley was riding in his horse drawn carriage with his wife, mother and four-year-old daughter when his horse suddenly took fright and ran away, smashing the front axle and wrecking the carriage. William Hellings and R.S. Fow were able to stop the horse, but not before Joseph Atchley was thrown out. He sustained severe bruises but miraculously no one else was hurt.[144]

John Provost had a Christmas fright when, on December 23rd, he was not only thrown from his wagon but his horse fell on him as well! He broke three ribs and a deep gash across his body as well as internal injuries. However, "at a late hour last evening he was reported to be doing nicely."[145]

Not everyone was lucky enough to survive a wagon accident. In the afternoon of Friday, April 30, 1915, Edward Cross, the six-year-old son of Joseph Cross, was run over by Charles Williamson's wagon. He was rushed to Mercer Hospital with serious injuries, though he was reported to be resting comfortably. Sadly, on May 3rd he succumbed to his injuries and was buried in Holy Sepulchre Cemetery in Hamilton Township.[146]

[143] Trenton Evening Times, January 3, 1896.
[144] Trenton Times, December 28, 1905.
[145] Trenton Evening Times, December 24, 1906.
[146] Asbury Park Press, May 3, 1915 and Trenton Evening Times, May 3, 1915; www. findagrave.com.

CHAPTER 14

AUTOMOBILES

MORE DANGEROUS, AND DEADLIER than the horse and wagon accidents, were crashes involving automobiles. Bigger, heavier, and faster and with poor road conditions, the slightest distraction could cause a devastating wreck. It was especially harrowing when the early noisy automobiles had to share the road with the ubiquitous horse and wagon.

The modern automobile was invented in 1886 in Germany, but it really was not until after the turn of the century that it started to become popular with the public, thanks in large part to Henry Ford and his mass-produced Model T.

The first known accident in Trenton Junction occurred on May 18, 1903. James Breese and Malcom Stewart were "automobiling along the [Old] River Road when their machine became unmanageable and ploughed into a bank at the road side. The auto was so badly damaged that it had to be carted to Trenton in a wagon."[147] While it is not known what kind of car this was, there were not many to choose from in 1903. Most likely it was a Ford Model A Tonneau, or something similar, with

---

[147] Trenton Times, May 18, 1903.

two seats up front and two in the back. It had a 2-speed transmission (plus reverse) and could reach a top speed of 28 miles per hour.[148]

Benjamin Baldwin, a grocer living in Trenton Junction, was upset by the article in the *Trenton Times* and its description of the accident. He found it to be inaccurate. He penned a letter to the editor, not only to correct the error but also to vent his dismay with the recklessness of young automobilists:

> SIR—I wish to correct the statement in the Times last evening concerning the wrecking of the automobile occupied by James Breese and Malcom Stewart. The wreck was caused by their running into the buggie owned by Clarence Jones who, with his wife, was returning from Trenton. [Breese and Stewart] were running at a very high rate of speed and recklessly turned their machine to the left side of the road, Mr. Jones having turned to the right and called them. They struck his wagon with such force as to break the shaft wheel and also the harness throwing the back part of the wagon entirely around. The horse being young became almost unmanageable. In striking the buggy they also ditched their automobile breaking it but the woman who accompanied them in the automobile said she was not injured. Women in this vicinity dare not drive upon the road owing to the reckless management of the automobiles—which are a menace to the lives of the people depriving them of the free right of a republic. In one instance recently a lady while driving was met by three automobilists and when her horse became frightened she begged of the parties to stop until she could turn out of their way, she was merely laughed at and the automobilists ran right on, the horse meanwhile bolting from one side of the road to the other, lifting first one hind wheel and then the other from the ground. The only respect shown by the automobilists was to order this lady to get out of their way.[149]

---

[148] https://en.wikipedia.org/wiki/Ford_model_A_(1903-04).
[149] Trenton Times, May 19, 1903.

Tragically, most of the automobile accidents reported in the press were fatal. A very bad crash occurred on April 26, 1904, on the Birmingham Road (Sullivan Way) heading towards Trenton Junction. George Holcombe, one of the best known newspapermen of Trenton, was killed and Captain E. Yarde Breese, of the New Jersey National Guard was severely injured, when Breese's car struck a rut in the road. Two other passengers, Hugh H. Hilson and R.E. Lacier, were only slightly injured. "The four men were hurled into the air as the vehicle was running at a high rate of speed. Holcombe was thrown against a tree and sustained a fractured skull. Breese was also knocked unconscious and may yet die from his injuries."[150]

Breese was driving his Winton motor carriage along the road towards Trenton Junction when they came to a curve. "Breese knew of the curve in the Birmingham Road where the accident happened and he steered to make it but failed to take into consideration that the rapid turning would swing the rear wheels of the machine to one side. The back wheels scudded into the ditch by the side of the road and in a twinkling the damage had been done."[151]

Breese was taken to Mercer Hospital where Doctor W. Keene, a renowned surgeon from Jefferson Medical College in Philadelphia, and assisted by Dr. Nelson Oliphant of Trenton, performed surgery on Breese's skull. "The operation resulted in the discovery that the inner plate of the skull had been fractured and a clot of blood that pressed against the brain was moved."[152]

Patrick Hines, a bridge tender "...stationed in the little settlement just south of the Reading Railway where he opens and closes the feeder bridge in the road from the river..." was hailed a hero by the press. He was returning to his home that fateful Sunday night "...when the toot toot of an automobile behind him caused him to swerve from the road with the bicycle he was riding and an instant later a big touring car dashed past. In it were four men apparently in the best of spirits and

---

[150] Philadelphia Inquirer, April 26, 1904.
[151] Trenton Times, April 26, 1904.
[152] Trenton Times, April 26, 1904.

heartily enjoying their wild dash through the darkness—a single light on the ponderous machine only partially relieved the gloom along the way."[153]

Just as Hines was about to turn down what is now Lower Ferry Road to head towards his home near the river, "his attention was attracted by faint cries for help coming to him from further up the road towards the Trenton Junction railway crossing." He peddled his bicycle further up the road and found the automobile in a ditch on the side of the road with two men weakly trying to move it but the other two passengers were nowhere to be seen—they were under the car. "They were Breese and Holcombe lying limp and unconscious and pinned down by the heavy machine Messrs. Hilson and Lacier were trying [to lift]."[154]

Hines tried to help but quickly realized that their efforts were in vain. He ran to the home of "some Italian laborers nearby" and asked them to help. This was no easy task since they did not speak English and Hines knew no Italian. But, he got the message across and, with their help, the car was partially lifted and Holcombe and Breese were moved to the side of the road. Hines then rode his bicycle down to the Asylum where he called for doctors and the police ambulance from Trenton.

The crash was investigated by John W. Howard, a well-known "automobile man." He discovered that the car was damaged as the result of a "fall and sudden stoppage."

> The tracks in the road leading to Trenton Junction "show that the machine was driven at the rate of twenty to twenty five miles an hour. The driver misjudged the turn in the road and steered directly into the open ditch that runs alongside of the road on the easterly side. The tracks show that the machine was given a turn of seven feet before the bridge was reached and in a straight path it ran into the ditch. This was about twenty feet from the bridge. At this

---

[153] Trenton Times, April 28, 1904.
[154] Trenton Times, April 28, 1904.

point the machine went off the road dropping five feet into the mud. The sudden stop was caused by the front axle of the heavy machine burying itself in the mud and then tilting to the right side. The searchlight on the machine was smashed, steering rigging bent seven inches forward, [the] top part of the dash board broke on the right side [and the] seat was broken. The accident was caused by the driver of the machine misjudging the distance and the turn of the road. He evidently knew the turn was in the road but either poor eyesight or lack of light caused him to make the fatal error. The steering gear was in good shape except for the bend caused by the fall.[155]

Captain Yarde Breese survived the crash. He was still unconscious, but slowly improving each day. By the second week of May, he had regained consciousness and was on a normal diet by May 9th. He was finally released and allowed to return home on May 24th, accompanied by a nurse. On July 10th, "Lieutenant E. Yarde Breese, adjutant of the Third Battalion" was well enough to visit their camp "in an automobile driven by his brother, James Breese." He continued to recuperate along the shore in Sea Girt.[156]

On January 13, 1913, Jonathan Strouse of Trenton was a chauffeur employed by Louis Gerofsky, a well-to-do grocery merchant in Trenton. Without permission, Strouse took his employer's car and arranged for a "joy ride," that included the Totten Sisters, Anna and May and, May Totten's eight-year-old daughter, also named May.

The adults had been drinking at a road house near Trenton Junction and, while driving back to Trenton along the Asylum Road, Strouse lost control of the car and ran into a telegraph pole. Young May Totten was thrown from her seat and suffered a fractured skull. She was taken to Mercer Hospital but doctors feared she would not survive her injuries.[157] Fortunately, it appears that young May did survive.

---

[155] Trenton Times, April 26, 1904.

[156] Trenton Times, April 26, 27 &, 29; May 7, 8, 9, & 24; and July 11, 1904.

[157] The York Daily (York, Pennsylvania), January 14, 1913.

Meanwhile, Jonathan Strouse was placed under arrest and on January 31st found himself before Judge Mitchell in the Mercer County Court. He pleaded guilty to taking a joy ride and was sentenced to State Prison for a term of two to six years "for driving an automobile while in an intoxicated condition and without the owner's consent."[158]

Exactly one year before this accident, five people drowned as the result of an automobile accident near the same spot where Jonathan Strouse ran off the road. A little further along the Asylum Road from the location of Strouse's accident site was a canal.

The Trenton Water Power Canal is all but forgotten today. It was a seven-mile canal built in the 1830s, along the Delaware River, around the same time as the Delaware and Raritan Feeder Canal that partially ran alongside it. The power canal drew water from the river by means of a wing dam at Scudder's Falls. The canal passed through downtown Trenton and emptied back into the river below the falls near today's baseball stadium. Mills were established along the canal that would use the flowing water for power. During the mid-nineteenth century, the Water Power Canal was one of the key components in the emerging Trenton Iron Company. By the turn of the century, however, only the Calhoun Street water pumping station was still using the canal as its power source. Today, most of the canal has been filled-in. The last remnants of it were lost when, in the 1950s, Route 29 was built on top of where the canal once flowed.[159]

On January 13, 1912, Frederick M. Foster's parents were away in New York City. His father, John, a wealthy manager of a worsted yarn mill, left strict instructions that his son was not to use the family car. Fred, a rambunctious 22-year-old decided to take the car out anyway. The fact that he did not have a driver's license did not seem to matter to him.

Along the way, Foster picked up friends to join him on his joy-ride

---

[158] Asbury Park Press, Baltimore Sun, February 1, 1913; Wilkes-Barre Record (Wilkes-Barre, Pennsylvania), February 4, 1913; The Leavenworth Post (Leavenworth, Kansas), February 5, 1913; The Review (High Point, North Carolina), February 6, 1913.

[159] www.hmdb.org/Marker.asp?Marker=4435.

about town: Chester van Cleef (21 years old), a car salesman, Alfred Donald Reed (21 years old), the son of former Supreme Court Justice Alfred Reed, Margaret Tindall (19 years old), the daughter of a Trenton fireman who lost his life in a fire, Helen Mulvey (17 years old), and Anna Hazel (17 years old), of Baltimore.

It was a bitter cold night with sub-zero temperatures. The friends were bundled up in "furs and rugs" and the tonneau was up with the side curtains were fastened.[160] At about 11:30 that evening, the party stopped at Louis Schmidt's Riverside Inn, located just west of Trenton Junction in Wilburtha, by the old Yardley Bridge. Schmidt said that he served two rounds of drinks: the first round consisted of three beers, one cocktail and two ginger ales. The second round was all beers and no whiskey was served. Foster drank at least one of the beers at the road house and Foster later admitted that he had several glasses of beer before going to Schmidt's.

The party only stayed at the road house for about a half hour, leaving around midnight. About forty minutes later, there was about pounding at Schmidt's door. It was Fred Foster, "half frozen and wholly exhausted." His clothes were "frozen to his flesh, his hair covered with ice, his hands and feet frost bitten." He staggered into the house and, after receiving "stimulants" explained to Schmidt that his car had been in an accident.

After Foster and his friends had left Schmidt's, they drove through Trenton Junction to the Asylum Road. Speeding along, when they reached the sharp turn of the road near the State Hospital, Foster, numbed by the cold, lost control and the car skidded about 50 feet. Foster applied the brakes, but they acted as a pivot, swinging the car around, plunging it into the icy water of the Water Power Canal.

Only Foster, who was driving, was able to escape from the car and struggle ashore. Schmidt called the police and Justice Alfred Reed was soon notified that his son was in an accident. Reed arrived at the scene about three o'clock in the morning and, once it was daylight,

---

[160] Tonneau is short for *Tonneau Cover*, the protective cover for the seats in an otherwise open car.

immediately took charge of the search for the bodies. It took most of the day to recover the bodies. Their bodies showed "terrible contortions" leading investigators to believe that "they fought desperately for their lives."

Two weeks after the tragic accident, Coroner Power impaneled a jury to investigate the deaths of the two men and three women. After four hours of testimony, the jury returned a verdict declaring "accidental death" and thereby exonerating Frederick Foster.[161]

The Water Power Canal claimed yet another life in June 1918. Harry Morgan, his wife and two sons—Donald and Harmon—along with their eighteen-year-old friend George Jones of Trenton Junction, were riding along the road into the Wilburtha neighborhood when the car's brakes gave out on a steep incline. Unable to stop, the car plunged into the Water Power Canal. Harry was able to rescue his wife and son Harmon, but was unable to save Donald who was trapped in the car when it sank below the surface. Jones, who was a poor swimmer, was unable to help and barely made his way to shore.[162]

---

[161] Asbury Park Press, Bismarck Tribune (Bismarck, North Dakota), Musklogee Times-Democrat (Muskogee, Oklahoma), The Ottawa Daily Republic (Ottawa, Kansas), January 13, 1912; Altoona Tribune (Altoona, Pennsylvania), January 15, 1912; Asbury Park Press, January 27, 1912;

[162] Harrisburg Telegraph (Harrisburgh, Pennsylvania), June 8, 1918. The road they were travelling down was either today's West Upper Ferry Road or, more likely (based on the steepness of the slope), Wilburtha Road.

CHAPTER 15

TRAIN WRECK!

WHETHER IT IS A form of Schadenfreude or some other psychological phenomenon, it seems that nearly everyone is fascinated by a train wreck. Maybe that is why people kept coming to Trenton Junction, because the Philadelphia and Reading line had their fair share of them!

The earliest wreck at Trenton Junction mentioned in the press occurred in 1885. A collision of a freight and coal train occurred just past the Trenton Junction station near the "Yardleyville" bridge, destroying an engine and several cars and injuring four railroad workers.

Shortly after midnight on July 3rd, freight train No. 653 was side-tracked at Trenton Junction when five cars and its caboose became detached and started rolling downhill towards the bridge over the Delaware River. None of the crew realized what had happened because they were all at the head of the train, save for flagman George McDonald. He had been sent to the rear of the train to flag any approaching trains while No. 653 was switching tracks. "By the time the detached cars passed McDonald, they had gotten under full headway, as the grade descends at that point ninety feet to the mile." When he saw the cars pass, he quickly realized what must have happened and "at the risk of his life and by great exertion he grasped a passing car, climbed up and set the break. By this time the cars had attained a speed of about forty miles an hour and his utmost endeavors could not appreciably lessen it."

Suddenly, McDonald looked up and saw the headlight of an approaching train—coal train No. 711. Running on top of the freight cars, McDonald ran to the last car and signaled the approaching train to stop. Engineer James Kinney saw the signal and immediately shut off steam to his engine, "whistled down brakes and waited to find the cause of the signal." Because the train was crossing the bridge, it was not going over eight miles an hour. Engineer Kinney saw the runaway train still quickly approaching so he "reversed the engine, put on all steam and started for the tender." This all happened so quickly that he did not have time to warn the conductor, who was sitting on the opposite side of the cabin in the fireman's seat.

When the collision occurred, the velocity of the freight train "… carried it up over the coal train and the caboose lay on top of the first car behind the tender. The engine was badly smashed and thirteen cars derailed, smashed and piled up in a mass upon the bridge."

George McDonald, the flagman/brakeman on the runway train, suffered from "contusions and lacerations about the face, scalp, and back…[but] was doing fairly well."

Peter Hawkins, the head brakeman of the coal train, was in the first car behind the tender. He was found lying on the platform of the caboose of the runaway train, just two inches away from the edge of the bridge and certain death by drowning. He suffered a contusion about the legs and other bruises but was otherwise uninjured.

Richard Brown, the conductor who remained in the cab of the engine unaware of what was about to happen, was trapped in the cab for three hours with another car on top of him before he was rescued. Both of his thighs were broken—a fracture of the right thigh and compound fracture of the left thigh. He was in excruciating pain "expecting every moment either that he would be killed while they were endeavoring to rescue him or that the train would catch fire and roast him alive."

Peter Kinney, the fireman on the coal train and the brother of engineer James Kinney, was not seriously injured and was taken home by his brother who was remarkably unscathed, having made his escape by running back over the coal tender.[163]

A few years later, another wreck was caused by a runaway train. A cattle car that was standing on a track at Trenton Junction somehow started down the incline towards the river. Once again, the collision was with an approaching coal car. The only injuries, however, were to the cattle who were badly maimed in the collision.[164]

The wrecks that occurred on the tracks between Trenton Junction and Bound Brook were, for the most part, freight trains. Apparently there were no injuries, with the exception of a fireman being badly scalded by escaping steam after "two heavily-loaded trains collided" between Belle Mead and Trenton Junction. The tracks were buried beneath a heap of coal and debris that took six hours to clear.

Darkness seems to be the cause of some of the accidents. This was true in January 1893 when a wreck occurred between two and three o'clock in the morning. A train of empty coal cars was stopped on a switch between Trenton Junction and the bridge crossing the Delaware River. "No lights were displayed from the rear and a freight train ran into it and piled up both tracks with empty cars." Again no one was hurt, but the tracks were blocked for several hours causing great delays for passenger trains.[165]

An accident reminiscent of the 1976 film *Silver Streak* occurred on January 10, 1909. A passenger train left Trenton Junction for Trenton. When it arrived at the Warren Street Station, the air brakes failed and the train crashed through the wall of the terminal station. "One of the passenger cars was thrown from the rails and the passengers were badly shaken up, but none was seriously injured." The engineer,

---

[163] The Times (Philadelphia, Pennsylvania), July 4, 1885; The Brooklyn Daily Eagle (Brooklyn, New York), Harrisburg Daily Independent, and The Decatur Herald (Decatur, Illinois), July 3, 1885; Steuben Republican (Angola, Indiana), July 8, 1885.

[164] Trenton Times, November 15, 1889.

[165] Trenton Times, March 7, 1887; Trenton Times, November 15, 1889; New York Times, May 18, 1892; Trenton Times, January 26, 1893; Trenton Times, May 17, 1904; Trenton Evening Times, November 30, 1906.

Richard Shiler, was badly injured; He jumped off the train when he realized that the breaks had failed. Howard Reed, the fireman, also jumped and was pinned beneath the wreckage but he was not seriously hurt.[166]

The deadliest wreck near Trenton Junction occurred on October 20, 1893. Just after ten o'clock in the evening, two freight trains collided about 150 yards from the Delaware River Bridge on the Jersey side, killing five people.

A long freight train carrying fruit was heading west towards Pennsylvania when it crashed into a coal train "a portion of which was standing on the west-bound track preparing to be transferred to a siding. The caboose attached to the coal train displayed white lights instead of the customary red signals, and the momentum gained by the freight train was too great to be checked in time to avoid the collision."

The crash derailed several of the coal cars and "telescoped the freight." Three cars fell down the thirty foot embankment, "breaking them into splinters....The tracks were torn up and bent into every conceivable shape and wreckage strewed the east and westbound tracks, making travel impossible for several hours...The freight and coal cars that were so badly damaged were set on fire."

It was known that several people were "stealing a ride" on the freight train; three of them were killed and four others were badly injured. Remarkably the engineer and fireman of the freight train were not injured, although they did suffer from shock.

On October 21, 1893, Coroner Coutier of Trenton convened a jury to inquire into the cause of the accident and to fix the responsibility it. The jurors went to the morgue to view the remains of those killed in the wreck and then went to the scene of the accident three days later. A Coroner's Inquest was scheduled for the afternoon of the October

---

[166] The Indianapolis Star (Indianapolis, Indiana), January 10, 1909.

24th, but the coroner decided that no inquest was necessary. He did not place blame on any of the trainmen or the railroad for the accident.[167]

Although there were (relatively) few train wrecks, and most of those did not resulting in serious injury or death, the same could not be said for passengers and employees that were around the trains. Trains are inherently dangerous and the number of injuries and deaths surrounding the trains of Trenton Junction is enough to make one wonder why anyone would set foot near the tracks.

---

[167] The Times (Philadelphia, Pennsylvania), The Trenton Time, The Evening Democrat (Warren, Pennsylvania), The Wilkes-Barre Record (Wilkes-Barre, Pennsylvania), New-York Tribune, October 20, 1893; Trenton Times, October 21, 1893;The Belvidere Standard (Belvidere, Illinois), October 25, 1893;Lebanon Courier & Semi-Weekly Record (Lebanon, Pennsylvania), November 1, 1893; Trenton Times, November 6, 1893.

CHAPTER 16

DEATH AND MAYHEM AT THE JUNCTION

Trains, though considered beautiful behemoths by many, are inherently very, very dangerous. They are massive. They are fast. And they were powered by high pressure steam. When around trains, whether passenger or employee, one has to be alert, attentive and careful. Even then, accidents do happen. And the railroad that came through Trenton Junction had its share of accidents.

One of first newspaper articles mentioning Trenton Junction (other than a train schedule), can be found in the *Philadelphia Inquirer* on April 17, 1876. It was a simple one line "filler" article mentioning that 36-year-old Joseph Dowdall who resided in Palo Alto, Pennsylvania, was an engineer on the Philadelphia and Reading Railroad. According to the article, Dowdall "had his right leg run over and crushed by a passing train, near Trenton Junction."

One of the most bizarre rail accidents involved the Secretary of State of New Jersey Henry C. Kelsey. On March 1, 1884, Kelsey was on his way to attend a meeting in Newark and had boarded the train from Philadelphia at Trenton Junction. He took a seat in the second car from the engine but the seat was too cold, so he decided to walk back through the train to find a warmer one. The train, said to be the fastest train in the country, was about a mile out of the station and just getting up to full steam, travelling "at least a mile or two a minute."

I had a newspaper and a pair of mittens in my right hand, and as I opened the car door I took hold of the brake wheel with that hand and put the other to my head to hold my hat. The train was on an embankment eight or ten feet high, and the wind had a full sweep across a wide field. It came in heavy gusts that rocked the car to and fro. As I stepped upon the platform one of these gusts came, and I was caught up and blown from the train. I remember trying to keep my hold on the brake, and then giving a great cry as I felt myself going through the air. I don't remember striking, but it seemed to me that I rolled over and over twenty times at the foot of that embankment along the track. I sprang up, and did not feel that I was hurt at all.

My first thought was for my hat and newspaper. I picked them up, and scrambled up the bank to the track. By that time the train had been stopped by a passenger who saw me fall, and it had backed up to where I was. The trainmen and passengers ran to me, and were sure I must be hurt. They wanted to take me back to the Junction and to send me home, but I insisted that I was all right, and climbed into the car again almost without help. They put me into a parlor car and fixed me comfortably, and I hardly felt hurt at all at first. At Bound Brook they wanted me to get off and have a doctor called, but I felt pretty well yet and would not do it. By the time the train reached Jersey City my foot was paining me terribly. I was beginning to be stiff and sore all over, and was willing to be put on a train for Trenton at once. I got back here at 11 o'clock this morning, and they brought me home in a wagon and carried me up to my room. My wife had not heard of the accident, and did not even know that I had gone on the train. A few minutes after I got here a telegram came to her from President Kelm of the Reading Railroad telling her of the accident...I don't think I am much hurt except my foot. That is getting more painful. I am bruised and sore, and am so nervous that I cannot rest, but the doctors say there is nothing serious the matter with me. I think my not being killed is owing to the fact that I struck on my feet first, and on the sloping embankment, so that I did not come down solidly all at once. I was muffled up in a heavy overcoat, too, and there was a little snow on the ground, which helped to break my fall.[168]

The chronology of train related injuries and death in and around Trenton Junction is extensive:

1884   On July 11th, Howard Fisk, a brakeman on the Philadelphia and Reading line, was crushed between the cars he was coupling at Trenton Junction.[169]

1890   Brakeman Harris Harbourt (considered an "old" railroader at the age of 25) had both of his thighs broken and his right foot badly injured while coupling two freight cars near the station round house. He was rushed to St. Francis Hospital in Trenton where doctors were not sure whether they would need to amputate both of his legs. "This morning they were making up a train and the brakeman was walking backwards with one hand on the coupling link beside a moving train ready to couple two freight cars together…He caught his foot between a "frog" or switch in the tracks and was knocked down and run over before the engineer was able to stop the train, even though it was moving slowly.[170]

1891   James Green, a wealthy farmer, was killed by a train at the Trenton Junction station.[171]

1893   In February, Eugene Shelby, a railroad employee, had his right hand severely crushed while coupling cars at the Trenton Junction Station. A portion of his hand had to be taken off.[172]

---

[168] The Sun (New York) March 1, 1884.
[169] Trenton Times, July 11, 1884.
[170] Trenton Times, January 25, 1890.
[171] The Montrose Democrat (Montrose, Pennsylvania), June 26, 1891.
[172] Trenton Times, February 13, 1893.

In September, Albert Boyle was found dying along the tracks a few miles west of Trenton Junction. The twenty-two-year-old Philadelphia native was struck by a train around eleven o'clock in the evening. He was found at 6:30 the following morning lying beside the track, unconscious, with a stream of blood trickling from his mouth. It was believed that he fell from an earlier train. He was brought on board a train heading for Trenton and the station telephoned ahead to St. Francis Hospital to prepare a place for him. "Another message was sent to the Central Police Station to have the police ambulance at the Warren Street depot upon the arrival of the train. Mr. George Muirhead, a passenger, who helped place the injured man on the train, accompanied him to the hospital." Examination found that Boyle had extensive internal injuries and died later that day.[173]

1896   On September 15th, James Zimmerman, a brakeman, was running along the top of cars of a fast moving freight train "and did not calculate the height of the Ewing bridge. His head struck the bridge and he was knocked off the car to the ground. A passenger train picked him up and brought him to Trenton" where he later died. The coroner's jury determined that Zimmerman died in the performance of his duty. "We also…find the company responsible for his death on account of not having their bridges of sufficient height for all employees to pass under with safety in a standing position."[174]

1897   On February 13th, Berrian Shafer of Wilmington Delaware and formerly of Mercer County, was severely hurt near the Trenton Junction Station. "As he came from one of the toilet rooms on a Philadelphia and Reading car he was suddenly

---

[173] Trenton Times, September 15, 1893; The News (Frederick, Maryland), September 16, 1893.

[174] Trenton Evening Times, September 15, 1896; Trenton Evening Times, September 19, 1896.

thrown against a seat, sustaining injuries to his back and side." He was confined to his bed for several days.[175]

On October 15th, William K. Ely "came to Trenton on a special." William Ely of Phillipsburg, New Jersey, was a man so poor that he could not pay his fare to Trenton on a regular train. So, he started to walk! He followed the train tracks and got as far as Trenton Junction when, at ten o'clock in the morning, he was "struck by the Reading Flyer No. 511." The "flyer" never stopped but word was sent to Trenton of the accident. William P. Rickey, Jr., "took out a 'special' train from the city which reached the scene in short order and brought the injured man to Mercer Hospital." He was still alive when *The Times* went to press, but he was in very serious condition and it was not known if he would survive.[176]

1898   At about 5:45 in the afternoon of September 18th, Mrs. Marcianna Harbourt, the 55-year-old wife of Uriel T. Harbourt, a retired farmer living in Trenton Junction just about where the Mercer County Airport is located today, was crossing the tracks at the Trenton Junction Station on her way home, having just returned from a visit to Trenton. While crossing, she was struck by an express train that was heading toward Philadelphia "at a terrific speed." She was struck before she could even realize what was happening. "Her body was thrown against a rail fence with such force that the top rail was broken. When the body was picked up it was found so mangled that it was brought to Undertakers Poulson & Coleman [in Trenton] in order to be made presentable. It was then taken to her home." It was believed that she started to cross the tracks not realizing that the train was approaching. Several people called out to her from the platform but it was

---

[175] Trenton Evening Times, February 13, 1897.
[176] Trenton Evening Times, October 15, 1897.

too late. "The engineer whistled loudly as a warning, but she became bewildered and unable to get out of the way" "The cries from the crowd only seemed to increase her fear, as she stood still looking at the big engine bearing down upon her." The Coroner Jury's verdict placed no direct blame for fatal accident on the Reading Railway Company. They said that "Marcianna Harbourt was killed by contact with train known as No. 527, while crossing the tracks of the Philadelphia and Reading Railroad at Trenton Junction…the train was not scheduled to stop at Trenton Junction and was running at an estimated speed of sixty miles per hour." The jury also pointed out that the railroad company had "no safeguards whatever at said crossing for the necessary protection of the traveling public."[177]

1900   Brakeman James Johnson was crushed coupling cars at Trenton Junction and badly injured. Recovery was difficult, but after a while he was able to return to work. In late 1901, he was "forced to take to his bed [and the] pain was so great that his mind frequently failed him." On January 25, 1902, his wife found him unconscious. He had committed suicide while temporarily insane" by drinking carbolic acid. "He was beyond human aid and died soon after being admitted to a hospital."[178]

1902   On February 24th, a Trenton Junction railroad employee had a narrow escape during a storm. A major winter storm hit New Jersey over the weekend, knocking down over two hundred telegraph poles between Trenton Junction and Belle Mead. "The village was in a very desolate condition Saturday

---

[177] Trenton Evening Times, September 19, 1898; Trenton Evening Times, September 20, 1898; The Hopewell Herald, September 21, 1898; The Goldsboro Headlight (Goldsboro, North Carolina), September 22, 1898; Trenton Evening Times, September 23, 1898.

[178] The Times (Philadelphia, Pennsylvania), January 26, 1902.

morning. The streets were full of limbs and some trees were blown down and the snow and slush was about two feet deep in some places...The men on the trains had to crawl on the cars on their hands and knees. James Callahan [narrowly] escaped injury by a wire, which came within a few inches of the top of the car. It swept him along the icy surface until he came to the end of the car and he fell down on the bumpers. He was dazed for a short time, but gradually recovered and escaped with a few bruises and a long deep cut on his arm." [179]

1903　　James McKeaney and C.T. Rosenbaum, engineer and fireman on a Reading Railroad passenger train were hospitalized in serious condition after the steam chest of their engine exploded. The train had just pulled out of Trenton Junction when an accident occurred to the main driving wheel of the locomotive, breaking the axle. The train was slowed down, but before it had come to a stop, the steam chest blew out, and the fireman and engineer were enveloped in steam. Before they realized what had happened, they were both terribly scalded." Train fireman Rosenbaum was so badly scalded it was expected that he would succumb to his injuries. His body was almost a solid mass of burns and it was believed that he also had internal injuries. Engineer McKeaney was burned and had several bruises but his condition was not very serious, although it was expected that he would be incapacitated for some time. Rosenbaum and McKeaney were the only ones on the train that received any injuries.[180]

1904　　On April 20th, air brakes failed on a train at Trenton Junction causing former Mercer County Freeholder John Reed and conductor McKenna to be "painfully injured." The train

---

[179] Trenton Times, February 24, 1902.

[180] Altoona Tribune (Altoona, Pennsylvania), July 18, 1903; New York Times, July 18, 1903; Trenton Times, July 18, 1903.

crashed into a freight car. The impact "hurled Reed over two seats and McKenna was thrown against the water cooler."[181]

Two months later, on June 6th, W. B. Fort's milk wagon was demolished at the Asylum Road grade crossing. Hiram Gilbert, an employee of Fort's, was driving home from Trenton after delivering milk. He fell asleep behind the reins and the horse continued walking along the road. When it reached the crossing, a coal train moving eastward blocked its path. The horse continued walking alongside the coal train with Gilbert still sound asleep in the wagon. Eventually the train snagged the wagon and wrecked it. The horse broke free and ran down the road, unharmed. Gilbert was knocked unconscious and removed from the wreck so that a doctor could examine him. He suffered a badly fractured arm, a broken rib and several bruises and cuts about his head and body.[182]

On October 27th, Charles Wade of Scotch Plains was crossing the tracks by the Trenton Junction station when he was struck by a steam engine and tossed into the air. As he came down he was struck again by the train and before it could be stopped it had run over his body. His leg and left arm were crushed and his left leg cut off.[183]

Another man was killed at Trenton Junction on the morning of December 15th. Henry Heidrick, "a stranger in this vicinity" and a friend were "in the act of jumping a freight, Heidrick on one side of the track and his companion on the other." Just as Heidrick was about to jump on the freight train, a passenger express train going in the opposite direction hit him, "hurling him forward and high into the air. As he descended he was hit again by the express engine and horribly mutilated. His

---

[181] Trenton Times, April 20, 1904.

[182] Trenton Times, June 6, 1904.

[183] Trenton Times, October 27, 1904.

right leg was severed and his body crushed and mangled." His friend had successfully jumped onto the freight train and he continued on his way not knowing what had happened to Heidrick.[184]

1905   Walter Callahan was a brakeman on the Reading Railroad. At about 7:30 in the morning of January 18th, he fell from the top of a freight car near Trenton Junction and broke his neck. He died just minutes later. When the train crew found him beside the tracks, he still had his lantern grasped in his hand. It was believed that Callahan caught his foot in a step on the train car and fell. His brother, John, was the engineer of the train.[185]

1908   Governor John F. Fort escaped injury when he was riding on a train that had just passed through Trenton Junction. Suddenly, the train stopped and the passengers were nearly thrown from their seats. "A broken rail had been discovered about a hundred feet in front of the locomotive and an automatic signal had flashed the danger signal upon the engineer so suddenly that he was forced to use the emergency brakes."[186]

1909   Barton O'Brien, a conductor on the Reading Railway, was riding in the cab of a train on March 14th. As the train passed another train at Trenton Junction, a piece of coal "…was hurled through the cab window, shattering the glass, pieces of which penetrated his eyes." He was taken to Norristown Hospital in Pennsylvania where he was to undergo surgery in an attempt to save him from becoming totally blind.[187]

1910   The Rev. George C. Boswell, a Methodist minister from Meriden, Connecticut, was killed instantly at Trenton Junction

---

[184] Trenton Times, December 15, 1904.

[185] Trenton Times, January 18, 1905; January 24, 1905.

[186] New York Tribune, December 16, 1908.

[187] Reading Times (Reading, Pennsylvania), March 15, 1909.

"...when he either fell or jumped from a train." The working theory at the time was that he was on his way to visit his parents in Ocean Grove, New Jersey. When the train arrived in Trenton Junction, he realized that he was on the wrong train. When he attempted to get off the moving train, he fell, struck his head and was killed instantly.[188]

Harry Thoms, a fireman on the Philadelphia and Reading Railroad slipped on the step of a moving train in Trenton Junction. His left foot went under one of the wheels of the train and was crushed. He was placed on another train and taken to the Prospect Street Station and from there taken to Mercer Hospital by police ambulance. His foot was so badly crushed, it was feared that it would need to be amputated.[189]

1911   Another Reading Railway fireman was injured—this time fatally—near Trenton Junction in the afternoon of May 17th. Howard Dennison was adding coal to the firebox of the engine when the draw-head gave way. The draw-head is a sheet of iron between the engine and the tender, or coal car. Dennison was standing on it, shoveling coal into the furnace when the draw-head suddenly pulled apart and separated the engine from the tender. "he was thrown down to the tracks and two cars passed over his body, severing his head and both feet and breaking one of his arms."[190]

1914   In August, Nicholas Morino was working on the Philadelphia and Reading Railroad, unloading a freight car when a log slipped off and struck him in the abdomen. He suffered serious lacerations and was taken by train and police ambulance to Mercer hospital.[191]

---

[188] Asbury Park Press, March 11, 1910.
[189] Trenton Evening Times, April 14, 1910.
[190] Trenton Evening Times, May 17, 1911.
[191] Trenton Evening Times, August 4, 1914.

1916   Mrs. Jennie Drayton, a seventeen -year-old African American woman was travelling from Trenton back to her home in Newark. She arrived in Trenton Junction and had to change trains. Unsure of on which side of the tracks to wait for her train, she crossed to the west bound tracks. Once she realized she was on the wrong side, she attempted to cross back "... when she became confused and stood on the track. A freight train was passing on the eastbound tracks and the express was approaching on the track upon which she was standing... The Towerman near the station saw the precarious position of the woman and tried to warn her but the sound of the freight train drowned out his voice. The Royal Blue Line express [of the Baltimore & Ohio Railway] struck her with such force that her body was thrown a clearance of about 130 feet and was badly mangled."[192]

1917   Twenty-three-year-old George Hanoch, a brakeman on the Philadelphia and Reading, died in Mercer Hospital a few hours after jumping from a freight train at Trenton Junction. He fell while jumping from the train and his left leg was crushed beneath the wheels of the train. Doctor Charles Waters happened to be out riding in his automobile with his wife and they were near the station at the time of the accident. He was flagged down and rendered first aid before rushing him to the hospital.[193]

1918   Harry Sexton, a member of a Virginia Infantry Regiment fractured his arm and received bruises when he fell from an early morning train near Trenton Junction. He was taken to Mercer Hospital to recuperate and his condition was said to not be serious.[194]

---

[192] Trenton Evening Times, October 13, 1916.
[193] Trenton Evening Times, September 22, 1917.
[194] Trenton Evening Times, June 29, 1918.

1919   Similar to Secretary of State Kelsey's accident in March 1884, it was in March 1919 that an unnamed fireman on the Baltimore & Ohio Train No. 9 was blown off his engine by high winds at Trenton Junction, "painfully injuring him."[195]

1920   Dominic Cucco and Sabatino Vagnozzi, both Italian laborers on the Philadelphia and Reading Railroad at Trenton Junction were instantly killed early in the morning of December 27th when they were struck by an engine as they were clearing snow from the cross-walks in front of the station. "The men apparently became confused when the engine appeared suddenly out of the dark. The accident occurred at 4:35 A.M."[196]

1925   Roy Herman was killed when he was struck by a train at the Trenton Junction Station on the evening of August 25th.[197]

1930   The last reported railroad related injury or death in Trenton Junction occurred on January 24th. William G.V. Haas, the chairman of the Ewing Township Committee, was killed when he was buried under several tons of coal while unloading coal car at a siding at the station. He was standing on a mechanical conveyer trying to dislodge frozen coal when he slipped and was buried when several tons loosened and fell on top of him.[198]

---

[195] Daily Courier (Connellsville, Pennsylvania), March 29, 1919.

[196] Trenton Evening Times, December 27, 1920.

[197] The Evening News (Harrisburg, Pennsylvania), August 25, 1925.

[198] The Brooklyn Daily Eagle (Brooklyn, New York), January 24, 1930.

CHAPTER 17

THEY FEAR THE CROSSING

SOME OF THE MOST serious accidents involving the trains at Trenton Junction occurred at the grade crossing on the Old River Road/ Grand Avenue. The treacherous crossing no longer exists, having been replaced by "the tunnel"—the steep dip in the road with a winding "S-curve" and a bridge that carries the tracks over the point where Grand Avenue now becomes Sullivan Way. The tunnel is located just a few yards west of the original grade crossing. [199]

On November 23, 1879, Thomas Luwin and J.J. Pierson were driving their horse drawn wagon across the tracks at the grade crossing. They were unaware of an oncoming fast train and they were struck. Pierson was badly hurt with internal injuries and Luwin "...was so badly injured that he cannot live." The two horses were instantly killed and their carriage was demolished. [200]

So dangerous was the crossing, that in 1894 the Philadelphia and Reading Railroad Company, who owned the tracks, found itself in Mercer Court on trial for "...maintaining a nuisance in an alleged

---

[199] A "grade crossing" is an intersection where a road or path and railroad tracks cross at the same level, as opposed the railway crosses over or under the road by way of a tunnel or bridge.

[200] The Brooklyn Daily Eagle (Brooklyn, New York), November 23, 1879.

dangerous crossing at Grade…" In Prosecutor Stockton's opening remarks, he asserted that the crossing was one of "extraordinary danger" because of buildings and in the summer, trees made it so that you could not see approaching trains until you were actually on the tracks. Also blocking the view were freight cars that were often parked on the siding right next to the crossing.

Samuel T. Atchley, who lived on his farm near the crossing for a dozen years, testified that "…trains go by with the steam shut off, because of the down grade, and without the ringing of the bell or the blowing of the whistle," thereby rendering the trains virtually silent.

There was a sign at the crossing, *Look Out for the Locomotive*, "but you don't know where to look for the locomotive!" And you had to look fast because trains travelling from New York ran at "a mile a minute." There was a flagman at the crossing during the day, but not at night and there were no gates. There was a warning bell that would automatically sound when a train approached, but it was "constantly out of order and there have been several narrow escapes."[201]

On August 7, 1904, The Ewing Township Council passed an ordinance demanding that the railway company install safety gates. The railroad took the case to the Court of Chancery where Vice Chancellor James J. Bergen, listened to testimony regarding the unsafe crossing and the township's contention that the rail company should install gates in compliance with their ordinance. [202]

The Railroad contended that the ordinance was invalid "…because it did not recite in its title its effect." They went on to further contend "…that the township committee [had] no right to order the railroad to tear up a county road in order to place gates at this crossing. It is said that a long trench must be dug across the road through the macadam in order to lay the machinery for operating the gates." The

---

[201] Trenton Times, April 23, 1894; Trenton Times, December 12, 1902.

[202] Prior to the re-writing of the State Constitution and restructuring of the government of the State of New Jersey in 1948, the Court of Chancery had jurisdiction over property disputes (as well as divorce cases and lunacy proceedings, but that is another story). The Chancellor was the chief judge presiding over the court and his assistant was the Vice Chancellor.

Vice Chancellor stated that the ordinance did not prescribe the type of gate and therefore it was not requiring the Railroad to dig up the road.

The Railroad called their own witnesses who testified that the crossing was *not* dangerous to the citizens of Ewing Township, "because trains were run over it at a greatly reduced speed. To corroborate the testimony of witnesses counsel offered in evidence an abstract of the train speed records at the Trenton Junction Station. Also offered was a copy of Superintendent Beach's order of February 26 [1904] stating that trains were being run over the crossing at too great a speed and ordering engineers and conductors to run their trains more slowly." The Township pointed out that this order only applied to freight trains. The Township also brought to light the fact that the Royal Blue Express of the Baltimore & Ohio line, which did not stop at Trenton Junction, passed the crossing daily at a rate of more than 60 miles per hour.

Trenton Junction resident John Tyman, a laborer on the railroad, testified that "...cars on the crossing could not obstruct the view of drivers attempting to cross the track. He declared that the sidings were sometimes filled with cars, but he did not consider that the view was obstructed. He admitted that cars had been stored there in fewer numbers since the commencement of the suit by the Township Committee." Tyman went on to testify that in his opinion, "...there was no difficulty in seeing an approaching locomotive over the tops of the coal cars, which were the only cars stored there. He declared that the warning bell at the crossing sometimes did not ring, but was always repaired within an hour."[203]

As of March 1906, nothing had been done to improve the safety of the grade crossing. It was so dangerous that the Trenton School Board allowed Ewing Township children who lived on the south side of the tracks, to attend the Dorothy Dix School near the Asylum, without having to pay the tuition required by city regulations. "The Dix School was nearer the families in question than the Trenton Junction School, and if the children went to the Trenton Junction School they would be

---

[203] Trenton Times, December 12, 1904; Trenton Times, December 13, 1904.

compelled to cross the tracks of the Reading Railroad. This was the reason they had been permitted to attend the city school."[204]

Another issue with the crossing was raised by the Trenton Street Railway Company. As early as 1902, plans were proposed for a new trolley line to extend from Trenton to Lambertville through Trenton Junction—and across the Philadelphia and Reading Railroad tracks. Because the trolley could not cross the tracks, "the plan which [met] the approval of every property owner within a radius of several miles from here is that the main road, Grand Avenue, be tunneled under the railroad tracks thereby avoiding one of the most dangerous crossings on the Philadelphia and Reading Railroad."[205] The trolley company wanted to bring the trolley into the heart of Trenton Junction. At this time, the trolley terminated at a point just south of the railroad tracks, and passengers were required to walk into Trenton Junction.

In July 1907, the Ewing Township Committee adopted a resolution "sanctioning the abandonment of the grade crossing on the Philadelphia and Reading Railroad west of the station at Trenton Junction." The decision was also approved by the Trenton Street Railway Company. Both the Street Railway Company and the Township Committee also approved a new plan "calling for a tunnel under the Reading tracks a short distance west of the present public highway crossing. The latter will be discontinued and the road will share the proposed tunnel with the trolley line."[206]

An issue blocking the abolishment of the grade crossing was the belief by some that changing the road would be too dangerous to automobiles, and some of the leading residents of Ewing Township were up in arms against the plans for the tunnel. E.V.D. Skillman, who owned the Skillman Hardware Company in Trenton, also had interests in Trenton Junction. In July, 1907, he was a vocal opponent to the scheme. "The driver and automobilist, going from Trenton Junction

---

[204] Trenton Times, March 2, 1906. After Ewing Township ceded the Brookville area to Trenton around 1900, the Brookville School was renamed the Dorothea Dix School.

[205] Trenton Times, December 12, 1904.

[206] Trenton Evening Times, July 11, 1907.

to Trenton by the proposed 'loop,' directly leaving the highway from a distance of 900 feet would be much below the grade of and very near parallel with the…tracks. He would be in total ignorance of what he might meet coming against him through the tunnel."

Around July 13, 1907, Judge Rellstab signed the order vacating the grade crossing "where the Asylum Road passes over the Philadelphia Railroad a short distance west of the station at Trenton Junction" paving the way for the tunnel construction. The plan was for the Asylum Road from Trenton to approach the Reading tracks "…in an oblique direction, so that south of the railroad there will be a very slight angle to reach the tunnel, which will be about 100 feet west of the present crossing. North of the tracks there will be a right angled turn to the east and then passing parallel with the Reading line the new road will join the old one and proceed into Trenton Junction."

Even with the judge's order, there was little progress made. In February the following year, a new schedule was placed into operation for the Trenton Junction Division of the Trenton Street Railway Company. Where previously trolleys left for Trenton Junction every 32 minutes, they were now going to leave every 27 minutes. The first car was to leave City Hall in downtown Trenton at 6:01 a.m. daily. The increase in frequency of trolleys still did not help get the tunnel built.

At the same time as the road issue, another crossing at Trenton Junction came under fire. Originally, the only way to cross from the east bound tracks to the west bound was by actually walking across the tracks. This resulted in several people being struck and killed by fast moving express trains. By December, 1908, the State Board of Railroad Commissioners agreed with the residents that the crossing was too dangerous and that either a subway or overhead crossing should be built, or at least a flagman present to help the passengers cross the tracks. The Railroad, however, disagreed that the tracks were dangerous. The Railroad did make some modifications to the station, but the locals said it was just as dangerous as ever.

Finally, in August 1909, plans were put forth for a rearrangement of the tracks as they passed the station, as well as for remodeling of the platform. "The most important change proposed is placing of a new crossing at the station. The crossing will be protected by gates, which will be closed whenever a train approaches. A fence is to be erected between the tracks of the main line, and an enclosed shelter for passengers will be built on the north side of the main tracks, with a new platform there. Thus, all passengers who are required to cross one track to take their train on the other side will have the gates as guards."[207]

Meanwhile, plans for altering the road crossing were at a standstill. In August 1914, the Ewing Township Committee complained to the State Board of Public Utility Commissioners and charged that "not only is the crossing dangerous at this time, but the population of the vicinity is growing and the section is rapidly developing with the result that the grade crossing is gradually becoming more dangerous. A large number of trains go through daily, endangering many lives. A franchise has already been granted to the Trenton, Hamilton, and Ewing Traction Company to cross these tracks with its trolley lines. Work has not yet been commenced on this crossing and before it is done, the township committee asks that the grade crossing be abolished and that the highway be either carried over or under the train tracks."

---

[207] Pedestrian gates were installed. However, even with the pedestrian gates in place, it was still dangerous for passengers crossing the tracks. On January 24, 1927, Mrs. Mary Carusallo and her two children, Mary (14) and Josephine (6) were visiting relatives in Trenton. As they made their way back home to Pottsville, Pennsylvania, they had to change trains at Trenton Junction. They ran under lowered gates so they could cross the tracks to board a train for the ride home. As they crossed, they saw a train approaching, and thought it would stop at the station to take on passengers. However, instead of being the Philadelphia and Reading local it was a Baltimore & Ohio express. The mother, who was ahead of the children, narrowly escaped being struck. However, when she turned, she saw her two children be struck by the express and hurled to their deaths. "The smaller girl's head was almost severed. The mother swooned and had to be given medical attention." She accompanied the bodies of her children back to Pottsville the next day. (Wilkes-Barre Times Leader, The Evening News (Wilkes-Barre, Pennsylvania), January 24, 1927; Lebanon Daily News (Lebanon, Pennsylvania), January 24, 1927; Pittston Gazette (Pittston, Pennsylvania), January 24, 1927.

By November 15, 1915, the editors of the *Trenton Evening Times* were becoming frustrated with the lack of movement on the tunnel project. Another conference was held in Trenton Junction and the newspaper recommended that if the conference failed to get anything done, then a grand jury and the courts should intervene. Fortunately, that was not necessary as the railroad company, trolley company and State Commissioner of Roads all agreed that the crossing needed to be abolished. "All that seemed to be required to put through the Trenton Junction tunnel project [was] the sentiment of the residents of the vicinity as to height and width of the improvement."

At the conference, Edward Katzenbach, counsel for the Philadelphia and Reading Railroad, said that the railroad company was ready to contribute $40,000 to the project and the trolley company was willing to contribute $10,000. The cost of a tunnel 40 feet wide by 14 feet high was estimated to be $70,000. It was assumed that the township would meet the remainder of the cost.

Four days later, it was reported that more than one hundred residents of Trenton Junction met at James Donald's house to discuss the tunnel project. Hervey C. Scudder was elected secretary and Samuel Atchley, the State Hospital Superintendent, was elected chairman of a group representing the local residents. He was to appoint a sub-committee of five to "obtain the opinion of the residents...as to whether the tunnel should be 40 or 50 feet wide and whether its height should be 14 or 16 feet."

The question of the width and height of the tunnel was of great concern to the residents of Ewing Township. Ewing was a rural community and "the farmers who cart hay to the city [of Trenton] seem to think it ought to be at least 16 feet high, as the present improvement roads have enabled them to haul much larger loads than formerly. The railway company contends that 14 feet is the standard required in Pennsylvania," which was where the company was headquartered.

In 1916, the tunnel still had not been built and the issue was now before the Board of Public Utilities. On December 19th, the "elimination of the grade crossing at Trenton Junction was assured...when the Board of Public Utilities...surveyed and approved the plans and agreement between the Philadelphia and Reading Railway Company and the Mercer County Board of Freeholders. The plans call for a tunnel just west of the present crossing 50 feet wide and with a clearance of 14 feet. They provide for a 30-foot roadway and sidewalks on either side of the roadway. The approach to the tunnel diverges from the present roadway just north of the Trenton Junction Schoolhouse on the Trenton Junction side of the railroad, and at a point on the lands of the North Broad Street Realty Company on the Trenton side. The grades leading to the tunnel will not be greater than 5 per cent."[208]

On February 28, 1917, it was reported in the *Trenton Evening Times* that County Engineer Harris had presented a report on his preliminary survey for the proposed project of altering the road in Trenton Junction. He estimated the cost of "...a sheet asphalt pavement at $25,553 and macadam at $15,460." Further progress was made when, in March, the State Assembly agreed to vacate a strip of land that was needed for the construction of the tunnel. Assemblyman Allinson, who pushed the bill through the Assembly, "stated that [the] property required was worth only about $100, but that the public would be greatly benefitted by the improvement."

The tunnel was finally built in 1918[209]. In May 1919, the Trenton and Mercer County Traction Company had completed the work of laying the connecting link of tracks at the tunnel and one month later, on June 6, 1919, it was announced in the *Trenton Evening Times* that the trolley service between Trenton and Trenton Junction was set to resume on June 7th.

It had been thirty-nine years since the tragic accident severely injured J.J. Pierson and claimed the life of Thomas Luwin and a quarter

---

[208] The board also approved the plans to eliminate the grade crossing at Ewing Station, currently the location of the Glen Roc Shopping Center on Scotch Road, just north of the Ewing Presbyterian Church. There was already a tunnel there as well as the grade crossing. "This tunnel at present is 20 feet wide and has a clearance of 9 feet. The company agrees to widen it to 33 feet and to give it a clearance of 14 feet." (Trenton Evening Times, December 19, 1916).

[209] There is no record of the actual date of construction in the newspapers. However, a cornerstone on the tunnel is dated 1918.

of a century since the Philadelphia and Reading Railway found itself in Mercer County Court on charges of "maintaining a nuisance" at the crossing. The tenacity of the local residents changed the face of Trenton Junction for the better. They knew in the nineteenth century that the crossing had to be changed. A generation later, and nearly a quarter of the way into a new century, their battle was won.

CHAPTER 18

THE WILD BLUE YONDER

Trains and trolleys were not the only forms of modern transportation to come to Trenton Junction. At the end of the second decade of the twentieth century, an airport arrived. But even before there was an airport, a plane had landed in Trenton Junction.

John Armstrong Drexel, the grandson of Anthony Drexel—the millionaire banker and founder of Drexel University in Philadelphia—was an aviation pioneer. On November 23, 1910, he set the world altitude record of 9,970 feet, just seven months after setting the previous world altitude record of 6,750 feet.

After setting his November record, he attempted to fly from Orland, Pennsylvania to Philadelphia. Orland is only thirteen miles from Philadelphia but he mistook the Delaware River for the Schuylkill and travelled north instead of south. After an hour of flying he found that he was over 20 miles off course. Short on fuel, he made an emergency landing in a field in Trenton Junction.[210]

It would be another eighteen years before an actual airport graced the landscape. On January 25, 1928, Governor A. Harry Moore switched on the beacon light at the southwest corner of the field that was to become Mercer Airport—"the first New Jersey link of the New

---

[210] Los Angeles Herald, November 25, 1910.

York-Atlanta air mail line." At the time of the lighting, the Mercer County Board of Chosen Freeholders was in negotiations with Hervey Scudder to purchase 208 acres of his land for the airport.[211] The location was chosen because it was "out of the fog area and located on the main postal route from New York to Chicago. [This] made the field available for emergency landings by mail planes" and would, hopefully, convince the postal service to contribute funds to the construction of the airfield.[212]

The airport was a grass field that ran 2,700 feet north to south and 2,370 feet east to west and sat at an altitude of 225 feet above sea level. The contract for the hanger was awarded to the J.H. Morris Company of Trenton for $36,050. Located on Bear Tavern Road, the hanger had enough space for 12 airplanes.[213]

A week after Governor Moore switched on the beacon, Clifford Carey, a farmer in Wilburtha, burst into the Governor's office unannounced. "Attired in overalls and [wearing] rubber boots," Carey was of the belief that the state intended to confiscate his farm for part of the airport. The State Police were called and a Trooper, in civilian attire, escorted Carey from the Governor's office. Carey, who also took the opportunity to air his grievances against aviation in general, was relieved to learn that he had been mistaken and that his farm was safe.[214]

The following year, in April 1929, just six months before the official grand opening and dedication of the airport, two men were injured at the airfield. William French, a pilot from Moorestown, New Jersey, was flying his plane while his passenger, John H. Lieb, a cameraman from New York, took motion pictures of a parachute jump made by R.E. Taylor of Lakehurst, New Jersey. At an altitude of 200 feet, French lost control of his plane and they went into a nose-dive, crashing into

[211] Asbury Park Press, January 25, 1928; *Images of America: Ewing Township, NJ.* JoAnn Tesauro, Arcadia Publishers, 2002, page 25.
[212] Trenton Evening Times, June 9, 1927.
[213] The Courier-News (Bridgewater, New Jersey), March 8, 1929; www.airfields-freeman.com/NJ/Airfields_NJ_Trenton.htm
[214] Asbury Park Press, February 2, 1928.

the airfield. French suffered a concussion and fractured both his elbow and ankle and Lieb suffered a compound fracture of his left leg and lacerations on his nose and tongue.[215]

The grand opening and dedication of Mercer Airport was held in conjunction with the commemorations of the 250th anniversary of the founding of the City of Trenton. At 8:55 in the morning of October 26, 1929, a battery of guns was fired in Stacy Park behind the State House, marking the beginning of the City's celebrations. The airport dedication occurred later that morning, followed by an air race that lasted the rest of the day. [216]

At 10:30 in the morning, Governor Morgan F. Larson led the dedication ceremonies. Shortly thereafter, races, stunt flying, and parachute jumps thrilled the 50,000 spectators who attended the event in Trenton Junction.

Many notable pilots and dignitaries were in attendance. It was "a brilliant crowd of notables...and internationally famous birdmen," which included Clarence M. Young, the Assistant Secretary of Commerce in charge of Aeronautics; United States Senator Walter Edge, Mayor Frederick W. Donnelly of Trenton, and aviators Russell Thaw, J. Wesley Smith, and Bob Hewitt, not to mention Clarence Chamberlain, Lieutenant Jimmy Doolittle, and the most famous "aviatrix" of the time, Amelia Earhart.

In the years between the World Wars, great advances were made in aviation. The pilots who gained their initial flying experience during the dog fights of World War I now turned to daredevil stunts, barnstorming, and aerial races to find excitement. Many contests were held worldwide and, on the day of the dedication of Mercer Airport, aviation contests abounded in Trenton Junction:

> Russell Thaw took first place in the contest for landing planes on the mark—a great white circle in the center of the field; Wesley Smith took third place in the 30-mile race for ships

---

[215] Asbury Park Press, April 8, 1929; The Courier-News (Bridgewater, New Jersey), April 9, 1929.

[216] Asbury Park Press, October 26, 1929.

with engines of 300-600 cubic inch displacement. Bob Hewitt, flying a Travelair powered by a 165-horsepower Wright J-6 whirlwind, came in first in the same race. His speed was 129.51 miles per hour. Second place...major Owens, flying in the 40-mile event for the John A. Roebling National Guard Trophy, cleaved the air at 137.79 miles per hour to win the first leg of the trophy, which must be won three times to become a permanent possession....The parachute jumping contest, which was won by Taylor, whose 'chute collapsed after he had struck the ground 95 paces away from the mark, was one of the most colorful events of the day. More than thirty jumpers hurtled into the air one right after the other. For several minutes the air was crowded with great silk mushrooms floating lazily toward the earth with tiny figures of human beings dangling on the end...Another exciting exhibition was staged by the Army's own crack stunt flier, Leiutenant Jimmy Dootlittle, who zoomed and turned and rolled on his back and did everything but nick a piece right out of the sky...More excitement was provided by three fleet Marine Corps planes sent up from Quantico, Virginia. They went through their paces, including the 'squirrel cage loop' until spectators were dizzy from watching. A squadron of huge bombing planes flew up from Langley Field, Virginia, and... staged an impromptu race of their own for the delectation of the thousands on the ground.[217]

There was a scare during one of the aerial races. As two planes were rounding the pylon at Titusville, New Jersey, "the wings of both planes scraped and interlocked...With controls damaged, the two fliers managed to straighten out the damaged ships and 'pancake' them to the earth. The ships were wrecked." Paul Rizzo of Barren Island, New York, who was piloting the lead plane, suffered cuts on his face and lost several teeth, however Captain R.W. Brown, of New York, who was behind him "escaped with a good shaking up."[218]

[217] The Philadelphia Inquirer, October 27, 1929.
[218] The Philadelphia Inquirer, October 27, 1929.

A year after the grand opening, another exciting event came to the airport in Trenton Junction. The All Eastern States Air Races were held on October 18 and 19, 1930. The event was sponsored by the American Legion Memorial Chapel Association as an attempt to raise funds for the construction of the *Cathedral of the Air,* a non-sectarian shrine at Lakehurst commemorating "the heroes of the World War and those who have sacrificed their lives for the advancement of aviation."[219]

Once again, famous aviators descended upon the village of Trenton Junction. Captain Frank Hawks, Lieutenant Alford Williams, Lieutenant Jimmy Doolittle, Bill Halslip, Bernt Balchen, Walter Hinton, Amelia Earhart, Elinor Smith and Duke Jernigan all came to participate in the prestigious air races. Even the US Navy's famous dirigible, *Los Angeles,* made an appearance.

The featured race on opening day was the 40-mile John A. Roebling National Guard Trophy Race, in which guard units from New York, Pennsylvania, Connecticut, Maryland, Massachusetts, Maine and New Jersey all participated. The 44th Division of the New Jersey National Guard was represented by Major Kellogg Sloan and Lieutenant John A. Carr. "The Roebling Trophy will be presented to the winner of the race by Adj. Gen. Frederick Gilkyson of the New Jersey National Guard at a dinner to be given Saturday Night at the Hillwood Inn, Trenton." The following day, the featured event was the "grand free-for-all race" that was open to all licensed pilots. [220]

Over 10,000 advance tickets were sold by Legionnaires, and more than 20,000 were in attendance on opening day. "All sizes and types of aircraft will be seen by probably the largest crowd that has ever witnessed an air meet in the east. In addition to the *Los Angeles*, and the navy Blimps, Captain Anton Heinen, German dirigible expert, will exhibit his recently designed air yacht, the first lighter-than-aircraft small enough for personal use. The Pitcairn Autogyro plane will also perform...The huge 24-passenger Burnelli all-wing transport piloted

[219] The Courier-News (Bridgewater, NJ), October 30, 1930.
[220] Asbury Park Press, October 17, 1930.

by Lou Reicherts will bring the officers and delegates...from New York to the meet."[221]

The first bit of excitement on opening day occurred when stunt flier J. Shelly Charles' Eaglerock aircraft collided with "21-year-old aviatrix" Nancy Hopkins. "Wind blowing across the field at thirty miles an hour gave the pilots trouble in bringing their fast ships down for good landings and cut down their speed in the air. A strong gust caught Charles' ship just as he was preparing to take-off to compete in the dead-stick landing contest, the first event on the program." The collision with Hopkins broke his propeller. Although there were no injuries, both planes were so badly damaged they had to be withdrawn from the races.[222]

> William Boyd, Jr., of Princeton, New Jersey, won the landing to the mark contest, his Avian's wheels stopping six feet, four inches from the mark. Park Reed, of Haverford, was second. The commercial race of 30 miles for 1,000-cubic-inch motors was won by Art Davis [of] Lancing, Michigan; George Zinn [of] Philadelphia was second, and Miss Marjorie Doig, [of] Bridgeport, Connecticut, third. The day was marked by an exhibition of stunt flying by Army, Navy and Marine Corps pilots, together with flights by autogiros, which flew to the meet from Pitcairn Field near Willow Grove.[223]

The air races and demonstrations continued the following day, and went without a hitch, until the closing event. "The crash came shortly after 5p.m. at the very close of the air meet, during the free-for-all pylon race," in which all licensed pilots were invited to participate. [224] As they reached the first marker and began their turn, George Zinn, Jr.'s Waco biplane suddenly clipped the tail of Robert W. Mackie's

---

[221] Asbury Park Press, October 17, 1930.

[222] Philadelphia Inquirer, October 19, 1930.

[223] Philadelphia Inquirer, October 19, 1930.

[224] The Morning News (Wilmington, Delaware), October 20, 1930.

Cessna monoplane. A reporter for the Wilmington, Delaware, *Morning News* described the scene:

> Death rode the wings of two speeding airplanes...a mid-air crash, 300 feet above the airport, viewed by the horrified eyes of 20,000 spectators ended the careers of two aviators. One gyrated to earth, minus the tail of his plane and was crushed to death in the wreckage; the other plunged down like a flaming rocket and only quick action of airfield employees saved his mangled body from cremation in the plane...It occurred about 2,000 feet south of the starting point of the race, where the throng was gathered. Both planes fell upon airfield property. A cheer arose as the contest started and Mackie sped ahead to be lead. Close behind him flew Zinn, fighting for flying supremacy. The cheer became a moan of anguish and a gasp of horror, a few seconds later, as the planes swept in wide arcs around the first pylon to the south of the starting point...A third plane flying close to Zinn offered danger of a collision and Zinn pulled up to avert this menace. As he arose the nose of his plane crashed into the tail of Mackie's plane, tearing away a section of it. Mackie's plane dropped into a tailspin as a cry arose from the crowd. Zinn, the wrecked tail of the other plane clinging to the front of his own, hurtled onward, back toward the throng, for a distance of nearly 300 yards. Then, about the cockpit shot long, withering spurts of flame and the plane plunged downward. Physicians rushed across the field to the wreckage of Mackie's plane. They found him dead. Virtually every bone in his body was broken. Fire apparatus...trundled to the flaming plane of Zinn. They managed to save his scorched body from annihilating fire.[225]

According to officials, Mackie and Zinn "...were killed because the low altitude of the crash, which occurred before 25,000 spectators, made parachute jumps impossible. Four ships had been closely bunched at

---

[225] The Morning News (Wilmington, Delaware), October 20, 1930.

the home pylon when Zinn, climbing to avoid one threatened collision, ripped into the tail of Mackie's plane."[226]

George Zinn, Jr., was 25-years-old and a wealthy sportsman of Rydale, Pennsylvania. Richard Mackie was 36-years-old, married and the father of two children. He started flying in 1916, during the First World War, and was an instructor at Kelly Field, Texas. For a short time in the spring of 1930, he was assistant manager of the Curtiss-Wright field in Valley Stream, Long Island before becoming a commercial pilot.[227]

In 1942, the Mercer Airport moved to its current location. At that time, it played an important role in the war effort. Avenger bombers were assembled nearby at the General Motors Inland Fisher Guide Plant. They were then taken by an underground tunnel to the Mercer Airport where they delivered to the military. 7,800 Avengers flew from the airport, including the plane George H.W. Bush—the future President of the United States—was flying on September 2, 1944, when he was shot down over the Pacific by Japanese anti-aircraft fire.[228]

---

[226] The News-Herald (Franklin, Pennsylvania), October 28, 1930.

[227] The Morning Herald (Hagerstown, Maryland), & The Reading Times (Reading, Pennsylvania),October 20, 1930;

[228] www.wikipedia.org/wiki/Inland_Fisher_Guide_Plant_(New_Jersey).

George Zinn (rear plane) and J.R. Mackie (center)
moments after their mid-air collision.

George Zinn's Waco seconds before his fatal crash.

George Zinn's Waco after his fatal crash at Mercer Airport.

CHAPTER 19

PUTTING OUT FIRES

TRENTON JUNCTION HAD A train station, an airport and a school. But it never had a fire department. It was not until 1947, that *West Trenton* established its first fire company on Wilburtha Road with just thirteen members.[229] That is not to say Trenton Junction did not have its share of fires. The worst fire, of course, has to be the one set by Robert Henson in November 1900. As discussed in an earlier chapter, Henson set fire to a house to cover his murder of Mary Elizabeth Van Lieu and her toddler son, George. He hung for that horrible crime in 1901.

In May, 1901, the "handsome Grand Avenue residence" of State Dairy Commissioner George W. McGuire was destroyed by a fire. McGuire and his wife took up temporary residence in the Trenton Junction Hotel. Fortunately, McGuire was insured. The following week, William Crozier, a representative of the Standard Fire Insurance Company, inspected the ruins and soon thereafter the insurance company settled with McGuire.[230]

Farms are prime locations for fires, with dry hay and improperly

---

[229] Tesauro, Jo Ann. "Images of America: Ewing Township, NJ." Arcadia Publishing, 2002.

[230] Trenton Times, May 23, 1901.

stored oleo,[231] wood buildings and sometimes faulty farm equipment. One area farm that was hit by fire was the Oakland Poultry Farm, owned by Ferdinand W. Roebling and managed by William S. Bowman. "Oakland Poultry Farm was one of the most extensive poultry farms in the area. One building alone contained over a thousand dollars' worth of valuable chicken of every breed [and] in the big orchard on the premises [were] many colony brooding houses."[232]

In June 1912, the farm was destroyed by fire. It was believed that the fire started due to a defective heating apparatus. Because there was no firefighting equipment on the farm, over three hundred and fifty young chicks were burned to death.

Alvin Temple's saw mill caught fire in 1904. Richard Corson noticed the fire at about four o'clock in the morning of April 30th and raised the alarm. Neighbors formed a bucket brigade which spared the mill from serious damage. While it was considered suspicious, no cause was ever reported.[233]

Just a few months later a bolt of lightning "struck and completely shattered a chimney" on the house where Express Agent George Tewer lived. "Several bricks were hurled through the slate roof and tin plates that were in the stove pipe holes were also hurled from their places across the rooms. The furniture was covered with soot." Balls of fire exploded in the house, filling it with blue sulphuric smoke and outside the lightning followed a rain conductor to the ground where it created a deep hole.

---

[231] Oleo is a term meaning oil. It is mentioned here because, in 1928, a devastating fire at the State Police Training School in Wilburtha destroyed their stables and resulted in the death of eighteen horses. It is believed that it was started by a recruit who was sneaking a cigarette in the middle of the night in the stables where the horses, hay, and "improperly stored oleo" was located. Once the fire started, it quickly spread, causing the barrels of oleo to violently explode. The fire was contained just moments before it reached the underground gasoline tanks.

[232] Trenton Evening Times, June 25, 1912.

[233] Trenton Times, April 30, 1904.

Mrs. Tewer was the only occupant of the house at the time. She sat at a table about six feet from the chimney. She was severely shocked and ran screaming into the back yard where she fell unconscious. Neighbors were at the scene almost immediately. Dr. Allen was summoned [and] the woman soon revived. Mr. Tewer was on duty at the station and as he was told of the affair he ran across the tracks narrowly escaping being run down by a fast express train.[234]

The following year, in November 1905, William Fort's carelessness nearly caused a disaster. The local Trenton Junction milkman was heating a can of paint on his stove. He was not paying attention to it and it boiled over, setting fire to his carpet. Fortunately, the flames captured his attention and he quickly extinguished the fire.[235]

The train station in Trenton Junction was hit three times by fire. The first time was in June 1902 when smoke was seen billowing from the clock tower. "By seeing it in time, it was extinguished without much damage."[236]

In 1903, the express car used on the train running between Trenton Junction and the City of Trenton was destroyed by fire. The fire was caused by a kerosene lamp, used for lighting the car, exploding. The local representative of the United States Express Company was unable to give an explanation as to why the lamp exploded. "It will take nearly a year to estimate the loss to the company caused by the explosion and fire, besides the loss of the car, which was burned to its trucks. It is known that several thousand dollars' worth of expressage was lost."[237]

A more serious fire occurred at the station in the winter of 1908. Old car barns that were once used by the Philadelphia and Reading Railroad as a paint shop burned on the morning of February 5th, causing a loss of $15,000. A $7,000 snow plow that was stored in the

---

[234] Trenton Times, July 12, 1904.
[235] Trenton Times, November 24, 1905.
[236] The Hopewell Herald, June 11, 1902.
[237] Trenton Times, October 17, 1903.

barn was also destroyed. "William Stewart, a railroad official, was painfully hurt. The origin of the fire is unknown."[238]

It was just before seven o'clock in the morning on November 26, 1915—the day after Thanksgiving—when William Paxson, a workman employed by the Philadelphia and Reading Railroad, happened to look up from his work. Across the way he could see the Trenton Junction School. It was an old brick structure situated on the lower portion of Grand Avenue, just across from the railroad. One hundred and fifty students were enrolled there, and it was on fire! Paxson immediately called the Fire Headquarters in Trenton and Assistant Chief Lanning "with the chemical" responded.[239] By the time the fire department arrived, "the structure was a mass of flames."

The Board of Education held an emergency meeting the following night in the Grange Hall to discuss finding new school facilities for the students. Colonel Frederick Gilkyson had recently purchased the old Weller Home in Trenton Junction and offered to rent it to the School Board until a new school could be erected. "The building which is a large and sanitary one will be fixed up temporarily today and will be thrown open for school purposes Monday morning."

A committee was appointed to look for a suitable location and to inquire into the cost of erecting a new school. Meanwhile, the old two room school building was sold to Vincenzo Falzini, a foreman working for the Philadelphia and Reading Railroad. He converted the building into a two dwelling home and added a second floor. It remained in the Falzini family until 1983, when it was sold to Weidel Real Estate.[240]

---

[238] The Washington Times (Washington, D.C.), The Evening Journal (Wilmington, Delaware), Alexandria Gazette (Alexandria, Virginia), February 5, 1908.

[239] The "chemical" was a fire truck carrying a fire extinguisher that used a combination of acid and soda to put out fires. "Sodium bicarbonate was added to the water in the tank and combined with sulphuric acid, which produced a chemical reaction that forced water from the tank into the hose…Chemical engines were used by firehouses until the 1930s, when water tanks with boosters became more common and expensive chemicals were no longer needed." (https://www.kovels.com/collectors-concerns/chemical-fire-engine.html)

[240] Trenton Evening Times, November 26 & 27, 1915. Vincenzo Falzini is the author's paternal grandfather. S

TELEPHONE 904-W

AMERICAN PLAN

TRANSIENT RATES, $2.50 PER DAY   ROOMS, $1.00 PER DAY
SPECIAL RATES BY THE WEEK

HOTEL READING
EDW. M. READING, Prop.

TRENTON JUNCTION, N. J. May 16th 1916

This agreement is made to day May 16th 1916
between V. Falzino first Part and
A. Machi Second part.
The Second Part agrees to do all the labor
work, Brick, as follows
complete two chimneys, raise the present
wall 5 feet, reset all windows frames,
And do all repairing for the old brick work,
This work shall be done in good Mechaical
Manner, The first Part agree to supply
all nessary material & pay the Sum
of 235.00 for Job. complete. payable
Every Saturday in proportion of work
done 80% per cent ballance when Job is
completed,

V. Falzine

Angelo Machi

Witness E. M. Reading

**Contract between Vincenzo Falzini and Angelo
Macchi for brickwork on the former Trenton
Junction School building. May 16, 1916.**

CHAPTER 20

THE LITTLE RED SCHOOL HOUSE

THERE HAD BEEN A small school house in the Trenton Junction area since the early days of the village of Birmingham. Known as the "Birmingham School at Trenton Junction," it was more than just a school, it was also a community center. In 1890, an entertainment program given by "the Birmingham School at Trenton Junction" was slated to "eclipse all former events of the kind." Musicians, including young vocalists Nellie and Fannie Trimmer of Yardley, Pennsylvania, were going to perform under the direction of Mrs. George Howell. The program was to consist of "recitations, dialogues, tableaux etc." The event was expected to draw a wide audience and it was announced that trains would leave Bound Brook "at 6:41p.m. and 7:28p.m., returning at the close of the exercises."

With the population of Ewing Township and, in particular, Trenton Junction, growing, an election was held on January 31, 1896, where it was decided by a vote of 102 to 13 to build three new school houses in the township, "one near the Asylum, one at Trenton Junction and one near Ewingville.". Bonds in the amount of $8,000 were issued to pay for the construction.

A tract of land was purchased on the lower end of Grand Avenue and a one-room school house was built, and later a second room was added. On July 2, 1903, a windstorm wrecked the school and a special meeting was held by the Board of Education. A vote was called for an appropriation of money to repair the school. The following May, 1904, with the population of both the Junction and the school increasing, the building needed to be enlarged by two more rooms. This made the Trenton Junction School a four-room school.

Sealed proposals were received by the Board of Education on May 25th "...for furnishing material and performing all labor necessary for the construction and completion of an addition to the school house at Trenton Junction." Each bid was required to be accompanied by a certified check in the amount of $300 "as a guarantee on the part of the bidder that he, if he be awarded the said contract will, within five days...enter into a bond and contract for the completion of said work by September 1st." If the contractor failed to sign a contract within five days the funds would be turned over to the Board of Education.

On June 2, 1904, a contract in the amount of $3,368 for the expansion of the school was awarded to Frank Sweeney. Board of Education members Joseph Arnold, Jr., J. Lincoln Knight, and Hervey C. Scudder were appointed to a supervisory building committee and construction began immediately. A contract was awarded to the New Jersey School and Church Furniture Company to supply the furniture in the new school. It was also decided by the Board of Education that the school would be furnished with steam heat.[241]

School was out of session, so classes were not interrupted, however church services and Sunday school classes that were normally held in the school building had to be moved to the Granger's Hall. Meanwhile, the Board of Education elected Miss Cornelia Cortor as the principal and Miss Verda Bowen as the primary teacher at the new school.

In 1906, many students who should have attended school in Trenton Junction instead attended the Dorothy Dix School near the State Hospital. The boundary of the township had changed and the

---

[241] They were able to afford the expansion, but the following year "owing to the failure of some of the residents of the Trenton Junction School District to subscribe money for the salary of janitor of the school, Allen R. Hullings has discontinued his work..." (Trenton Times, April 25, 1905.

Brookville Section of Ewing Township where the Dix school was located was ceded to the City of Trenton. The City, however, allowed the students from Ewing to continue attending the Dix School without having to pay the non-resident tuition fee because of the danger in crossing the train tracks in Trenton Junction. By the start of the new school year in September 1906, the students were expected to attend Trenton Junction, which increased attendance by nearly 60 students.

There was a complaint by the teachers throughout Ewing Township in 1906 concerning "irregular attendance." It was believed to be due to a general disinterest of the parents. "This year, the school directors will post notices throughout the township to parents and guardians quoting extracts of the school law in reference to the attendance of children between the ages of seven and fourteen years. The school board will enforce this law."

To assist with improving attendance, the schools began publishing monthly reports in the newspaper listing the percentage of attendance for each school and the names of "...pupils neither absent nor tardy." It became a source of inspiration and pride for the students to attend class and help keep the percentages up in comparison to their rival schools and it was quite naturally exciting to see their names listed in the newspaper!

In February 1908, a gift was made to the Trenton Junction School by Washington Camp No. 7 of the Patriotic Order Sons of America. The group presented a flag and a Bible, with the inscription "Trenton Junction Public School, Presented by Washington Camp No. 7, P.O.S. of A."

The members of the camp were met at Trenton Junction by a delegation of twenty-five boys and girls, "bearing American flags, who escorted them to the Borough Hall, which was crowded with the parents and friends of the children. Professor Thomas M. White made the presentation speech. On behalf of the school the flag and Bible were received by Superintendent of the School Board Scovel... [and] refreshments were served during the evening."

Another source of pride for the school came the following year in January, 1909, when Joseph Arnold, Jr., "gave a short address in which he congratulated the teachers on behalf of the parents, upon the interest they had taken in securing [a] piano...The Trenton Junction School [was] the only school in Ewing Township that [had] a piano."

Most assuredly this piano played a part in the celebrations of Washington's Birthday that year. Today, the First President's birthday is noted by shopping and sales around the country. But in the early part of the century, Washington was commemorated a bit differently:

> An entertainment in celebration of Washington's Birthday was held last evening in the Grand Conservatory of Music and Languages, at Trenton Junction. There was a large attendance of students and their friends and relatives and the event was a very successful one. Miss Dorothy Thompson and Miss Ina Carey gave violin selections. Miss Mabel Rittenhouse gave a recitation on 'The Immortal Washington.' Miss Sara Weller gave a piano solo. Miss Anita McKerney gave a recitation. Miss Sarah Weller gave reproduction of the life of Washington. Similar reproductions are given by the pupils every Friday. Miss Mabel Rittenhouse gave a piano solo. Miss Lillian Doyle gave 'The Little Hatchen' by Robert Burdette, while J. Stewart Hill gave a violin solo. Miss May Skillman gave a recitation entitled 'She Danced with Washington.' Miss Alice Reynolds also gave a recitation. The following gave a minuet as it was danced in Washington's time: Miss Mabel Rittenhouse, Miss Anita McKerney, Miss Sara Weller, Miss Lou Weller, J. Stewart Hill, I. Furman Blackwell, Newton A.K. Bugbee, Jr., and J. Newell Holcombe. The characters portrayed were Goddess of Liberty, Miss May Skillman; Columbia, Miss Mabel Rittenhouse; Peace, Miss Lillian Doyle; America, Miss Alice Reynolds. The entertainment was brought to a close by the singing of the Star Spangled Banner.[242]

Unfortunately, not everything was idyllic at the Trenton Junction School. At least not in 1911 when Professor Newton Wyckoff, a teacher

---

[242] Trenton Evening Times, February 23, 1909.

at the school, appeared before Justice of the Peace William S. Mills in Trenton and charged William Rudolph Stokes of Trenton Junction with assault and battery! A warrant was then issued for the arrest of William Stokes.

Mabel L. Stokes, the younger of two children of William Rudolph and Elizabeth Stokes, was 15-years-old in 1911 and was a student at the Trenton Junction School. According to her aunts, Anna and Ethel Stokes of Morrisville, Pennsylvania, Mabel had "been always considered a very bright scholar and [was] never hard to manage, as her other teachers can testify." However, her teacher in this particular year felt otherwise. Professor Newton claimed that she had trouble and was "backward in her studies and incorrigible."

On Friday, June 16, 1911, Professor Newton said Mabel had become unmanageable and he sent her home from school. She refused to go, so Newton "opened the door and insisted on her going." She did, but when she got home she told her father that her teacher had struck her "twice in the face." This news infuriated the girl's father and he went to the school on Grand Avenue and "attacked the teacher, striking him in the face, tearing his collar and otherwise misusing him." He then threatened to "lay [in wait] him and beat him up" when he left the building.

Adding to the fray, Mabel's mother, Elizabeth, wrote a letter to the editor of the *Trenton Evening Times* that appeared on June 27th. She claimed that Wyckoff's statements about her daughter were false and that she found it "a very surprising thing that Mr. Wyckoff should make such false statements against a young girl and take advantage of her because he has had trouble with her father." According to Mrs. Stokes, no one in the three grades that Professor Wyckoff taught was promoted to the next grade level that year. "All the mothers who have children in Mr. Wyckoff's grades, especially those who have children in the eighth grade, feel very disappointed that no one was promoted. It is impossible that the blame lies wholly with the children."

After this dramatic build-up in the newspapers, the story vanishes. There is no mention of the outcome—what happened to William Rudolph Stokes? And what happened to Mabel? Was Professor Wyckoff held accountable for all three grades allegedly not being promoted?

According to the 1920 Census, the Stokes family had moved to Trenton, but it is not known when. Is it possible that they decided to move so that their daughter could attend school in the city rather than in Trenton Junction? Unfortunately, the records have yet to be discovered that can answer these questions.[243]

Another item that is difficult to research concerns the *other* school in Trenton Junction at the turn of the century. Ira, Verde and Maude Bowen were teachers living in Trenton Junction with their mother. In 1904, Verda was one of the teachers in the Trenton Junction School. Sometime prior to 1908, the sisters opened a non-sectarian private school "at their home in Trenton Junction with ten pupils." It was a "home and day school" teaching primary through college preparation. According to an advertisement for the school in the June 28, 1912 issue of the *Trenton Evening Times*, "special advantages in music may be secured at this school, and day and boarding pupils are prepared for any school desired." According to the New York Times, boys were admitted "in all departments except the advanced."

In 1913, the school had moved to 214 West State Street in Trenton when it merged with a very well-known day school in Trenton that was run by Catalina Van Cleef. The school was briefly known as the Bowen-Van Cleef School.

Two years after the Bowen school left Trenton Junction, on the day after Thanksgiving in 1915, a great fire destroyed the four-room Trenton Junction School. From the time of the fire in November 1915 until October 1916, the Board of Education rented a private residence to use as a temporary school. Immediately after the fire, the school board appointed a special committee to recommend a location for a new school. It was decided not to rebuild on the old site on Grand Avenue because the proximity to the railroad—"the noise from passing trains [was] a great nuisance in the class rooms." In addition to the special committee, the residents of Trenton Junction called for a meeting in early December that was held in the Grange Hall to discuss the matter of the school's relocation and construction.

---

[243] June 19, 1911, June 23, 1911; June 27, 1911, Asbury Park Press, June 22, 1911.

A special election was held the following April "in the Lanning School between the hours of 4 and 8 o'clock" on April 25th to decide the issue of granting Trenton Junction an additional bond of $9,000 for the rebuilding of the school. "There were 378 ballots polled at the election, and of this number 191 were for the bond issue and 184 against it, with three votes rejected." With the passage of the bond, the Board of Education now had a total of $38,000 available for the new Trenton Junction School. "Of this sum, $25,000 was authorized by a previous special election; $4,000 is in hand from insurance on the old building, and $9,000 granted by yesterday's election."

The special bond election was considered one of the "most spirited school elections Ewing Township has ever known." The passage came as a surprise to many, as it was believed that there would be little or no opposition to the issuance of the bond. One hundred years later, a national election in 2016 would be among "the most spirited" elections the nation had ever known with an outcome that "came as a surprise to many."

Although not granted the right to vote in national elections until four years later, approximately 100 women voted in the bond election and it was estimated that 75 percent of them voted in favor of passage. "The votes from Trenton Junction carried the day for the bond issue, for practically every man and woman from there who voted were in the affirmative."

In March 1916, William and Bertha Fisk deeded their land on Ewing Avenue to the Board of Education for the school. The school was due to open in October 1916, but was delayed six weeks "...due to an infantile paralysis epidemic." On April 19, 1917, the new Trenton Junction School was renamed "Fisk Elementary School" in honor of the land benefactors.[244]

The only school that was in existence during the "Trenton Junction

---

[244] Trenton Evening Times, April 18, 1896, June 8, 1896; February 6, 1908, February 27, 1909, February 23, 1909, May 26, 1909, June 28, 1912;Trenton Times, July 10, 1903, May 9, 1904, May 21, 1904, June 2, 1904, June 4, 1904, June 14, 1904, August 30, 1906; New York Times, July 6, 1913; November 30, 1915, April 25, 1916; "A Handbook of American Private Schools," 4th Edition, Porter E. Sargent, Geo. H. Ellis Co., Boston, 1918; "Patterson's American Educational Directory," Volume 11, Homer L. Patterson, American Educational Company, Chicago, 1917.

Years" that is still in existence today is the New Jersey School for the Deaf. Established in 1883 "at an old facility for orphaned children of Civil War soldiers on Hamilton and Chestnut Avenues," the State of New Jersey purchased 100 acres of the Scudder Farm on Sullivan Way and construction was begun on a new campus. [245] In 1923, the Primary Unit opened. An additional $502, 200 was appropriated for additional construction. In October, 1924, the general contract was awarded to Victor Gonday of Philadelphia[246].

The Middle and Upper Units opened in 1926. The primary unit building was topped by the famous clock tower. Built in 1922, the clocks were not installed until 1952, when they were dedicated by Mary Pope to the memory of her late husband, Dr. Alvin E. Pope, who served as superintendent from 1917-1940. [247]

In the 1920s, the "oral method of instruction where classes are conducted by speech and speech reading is used in all cases except a few...In the industrial department, courses are given in printing, including hand composition, presswork, linotype operating and photo engraving. There are excellent courses in wood and metal trades for the boys; dressmaking, millinery and cooking for the girls. After the pupils finish the grammar school course they are privileged to complete their trades or prepare for Gallaudett College."[248]

On March 22, 1965, the school was renamed the Marie H. Katzenbach School for the Deaf. Marie Katzenbach was a member of the New Jersey State Board of Education. She served on the board for 43 years and was a steadfast advocate for the school, its students and New Jersey's deaf community at large.

Nearly a century after moving to Trenton Junction, the Katzenbach School remains an integral and important West Trenton institution.

---

[245] Jo Ann Tesauro, "Images of America: Ewing Township, NJ," Arcadia Publishers, 2002, page 45.

[246] Courier-News, Bridgewater, New Jersey, July 15, 1924; Asbury Park Press, October 24, 1924

[247] NJSD Katzenbach School News, Vol. 84, No. 2, Winter 2016, page 11.

[248] www.mksd.org/about.htm; Philadelphia Inquirer, December 15, 1928.

CHAPTER 21

THE OLD FOUNDRY

IN THE SPRING OF 1893, when Jacob Kurtz was busy building his new hotel in Trenton Junction, the Wilbraham Brake & Power Blower Company was expected to start their operation. Their factory was a 50 by 500 foot brick building with a 2,900 square foot slag roof, located along the Philadelphia and Reading Railroad tracks near the station.[249]

The Power Blower Company did not last long in Trenton Junction, and the factory was soon abandoned. Just shy of a decade later, in January 1902, it was announced in the *Trenton Times* that the "old foundry at Trenton Junction" was going to be occupied by "a new enterprise." This "new enterprise" was an automobile factory. Twenty carloads of ashes were spread out in a six-inch layer on the floor, and this was reinforced by several layers of plank and concrete in order to stand the weight of the heavy machinery that was going to be installed.

The paper stated that a "large force of men will soon be employed." They would initially live in Trenton and then, once houses were built, they would move into Trenton Junction. In March 1902, the Diebold Cox Manufacturing Company sued Walter M. Hess of the automobile company that was moving into the old foundry, "to recover on a lot of machinery supplied to the automobile company which has not yet put

---

[249] Trenton Times, March 28, 1893; Hagley Digital Archives: digital.hagley.org/.

its plant in operation." The State Supreme Court granted an additional $5,000 attachment to the suit against Walter M. Hess of the automobile company.

It is not known what automobile manufacturer this was or if it even opened for business. There was, however, an automobile factory in the building in 1915: "Taxicabs and touring cars, changeable bodies for taxicabs, some almost new, can be seen at [the] Factory Building in Trenton Junction…" Additionally, a 1918 road map identifies the "American Motor Car Manufacturing Company" in Trenton Junction. The American Motor Car Manufacturing Company was a short-lived car manufacturing company based in Indianapolis, Indiana. Founded in 1906, it went into receivership in 1913.

After the American Motor Company went out of business, the massive factory building was used by the State Highway Department to store a few "Bull Dog Mack Trucks," but for the most part, it was left abandoned for nearly twenty years. So, the local children of Trenton Junction would play in the building during inclement weather. "It was like a gymnasium!" They would play baseball in there, throwing rocks through the windows. The windows were reinforced with chicken wire, "…so we'd practice throwing rocks through the holes in the wire. That's how we practiced our pitching for baseball. That's why we were so good."[250]

Because the foundry had a concrete floor, the children would roller skate on it. "There used to be an old car – just a frame and four wheels – and we used to push that around in there. Man it was dirty in there! There were great big beams up on the ceiling that were falling down. We're lucky they didn't fall on us!" [251]

The next documented occupant of the building came in the 1930s. Tyler Winner's company "began building boats and related water sports equipment in the early thirties." Originally located at 623 Prospect Street in Trenton, the company relocated to the former car manufacturing building in Trenton Junction. *Winner Manufacturing*

[250] Garzio, John "Jake". *Interview with the author.* May 12, 1991.
[251] Falzini, Michael J. *Interview with the author.* May 12, 1991.

thrived as one of the major employers of Trenton Junction residents, second only to the General Motors plant that arrived nearby at the end of the 1930s. After World War II, *Winner Manufacturing* expanded into fiber glass products and remained a vital part of the area until the company filed for bankruptcy in the mid-1970s. The old factory building was torn down in the early 1990s.[252]

[252] Trenton Times, March 28, 1893, January 18, 1902, January 27, 1902, March 19, 1902; Trenton Evening Times, June 30, 1915; *Yachtsmen's Magazine: Motor Boating*, June 1939, page 104; fiberglassics.com/library/File:Winnerhist.jpg. The Winner Company was reorganized as the Wehco Plastics, Inc. in 1974 and shortly thereafter the company filed for bankruptcy. The company's pension fund was "lost" and pension benefits terminated on December 10, 1975. The Pension Benefit Guaranty Corporation trusteeship began on July 8, 1976, and provided pension benefits to 104 participants. (www.pbgc.gov).

The Old Foundry at Trenton Junction.

CHAPTER 22

PRÆDICANS AD CONFLUENTES[253]

IN 1905, TRENTON JUNCTION had a most exotic visitor, from far away Nagaland, a province found in the jewel of the British Empire's crown, India. Located in the northeastern corner of that country, Nagaland borders Burma and it is one of modern India's smallest states. Surrounded by Hinduism and Buddhism, Nagaland is mostly (88 percent) Christian.

Around 1887, a boy named Eramo Shanjamo Jungi was born in Nagaland. He was of the Lota tribe and, in 1905, he became the first Naga to come to the United States and receive a foreign education.

Mrs. S.A. Parrine was the wife of a Baptist minister and the daughter of Rev. and Mrs. M.T. Lamb of Grand Avenue, in Trenton Junction. She and her husband were Baptist missionaries sent to Nagaland. On December 27, 1904, they brought Shanjamo back to the United States. He spent 1905 living with the Lambs in their farmhouse on Grand Avenue, and he spent the school year studying at the Trenton Junction public school, just down the road.

On October 27, 1905, the Rev. Judson Conklin, of the Clinton Avenue Baptist Church in Trenton, arranged to have Shanjamo lecture about his home. Mrs. Parrine interpreted for him.

---

[253] Latin for: *Preaching at the Junction*

The following year, Shanjamo transferred to a school in Port Norris and finally, in 1907, he transferred to the Mt. Hermon School in Warren County. He returned to Nagaland on November 27, 1908. He was very active in the Baptist Church in India, was ordained, established churches and preached at many churches throughout his homeland. He died in 1956.

Today in Nagaland, there is a monument to Eramo Shanjamo Jungi, highlighting the fact that he was the first of his people to receive a foreign education. On the monument is a plaque with his photograph and a list of all of his accomplishments in life and as a Baptist minister and missionary. Included in this vast list is his stay in Trenton Junction.[254]

Religion was a very important component of life in Trenton Junction at the turn of the century. The first European settlers in the area were Baptists, Presbyterians and Episcopalians. The Roman Catholic population was very tiny until the advent of the railroads— and the arrival of immigrant railroad workers from Italy.

Initially, there was no actual church building in Trenton Junction for any religion. Episcopalians met in private homes, usually after seven o'clock on Sunday evenings. They never developed more than a mission in Trenton Junction, which was known as *St. Alban's Mission*. The closest Episcopal Church was built on Prospect Street in Ewing Township after the turn of the century.

The origin of the Presbyterian Church in Trenton Junction stretches back to 1845 when the church was initially organized as the *Birmingham Sunday School*. At that time, classes were held "in the old stone school house" and were directed by the Rev. Eli Field Cooley of Ewing Presbyterian Church.

When the railroad arrived in 1876, and Birmingham was renamed Trenton Junction, the Sunday School was also renamed the *Trenton Junction Sunday School*. It was not until 1906 when the school was

---

[254] Falzini, Mark. *West Trenton's Connection to* India. Archival Ramblings. September 2016. http://njspmuseum.blogspot.com/2016/09/west-trentons-connection-to-india.html.

incorporated as the Trenton Junction Community Church. At that time, "Grange Hall on Grand Avenue was purchased and used for Sunday School and Church purposes."

In 1918, property on the corner of Grand and Trenton Avenues was donated by Trenton attorney, Isaac Richey, for use as a church site. The following year, "the congregation bought additional adjoining property." It would still be more than a decade before an actual church building would be erected.

When the new Trenton Junction train station changed its name to West Trenton, so too did the West Trenton Presbyterian Church. In April 1931, a Loyalty Campaign was begun to help raise the $25,000 needed for the construction of a permanent stone church. Throughout the month of April, special prayer services, meetings and lectures, and dinners were held to raise additional funds.

Construction finally began in May. The church was "a brownstone structure of Norman Gothic architecture, with a belfry, bell, and cathedral windows. The bell was presented to the church by the Ladies' Aid Society in 1932." The new church had enough seating for 150 congregants. A church hall was also built, with Sunday School rooms located in the basement. Services began being held in the church in October 1932.[255]

When the Italian immigrants moved into Trenton Junction to work on the railroad, there were no Roman Catholic churches nearby. They would take the trolley into Trenton to attend Mass at St. Joachim's Church—Trenton's Italian parish.

In 1915, Joseph Croce asked the diocese to send a priest to Trenton Junction. The Bishop of Trenton agreed, and he assigned a priest to celebrate Mass each Sunday at six o'clock in the morning on Croce's porch. Unfortunately, during inclement weather, Mass was cancelled.[256]

---

[255] "Inventory of the Church Archives of New Jersey: Presbyterians." Newark, NJ: The Historical Records Survey, 1940; Trenton Evening Times, April 3, 1931.

[256] Tesauro, JoAnn. "Images of America: Ewing Township, New Jersey." Arcadia Publishers, 2002, page 40.

Nuns were dispatched from St. Joachim's to instruct the children in Catechism and prepare them for Confirmation.

An empty building owned by Frank Roma of Philadelphia that was located in the center of the railroad camp was secured and converted into a makeshift church. "It was a tin garage and was heated by a potbellied stove. In the summer, the doors were left open and goats and chickens would wander in during Mass." The first Mass was celebrated in the new church on Palm Sunday, April 24, 1918.

Eventually, the congregation outgrew the makeshift church. Sometime in the 1930s, a new parish church, Our Lady of Good Counsel, was built on Grand Avenue, just north of Summit Avenue, where the Post Office is currently located. In 1963, the parish moved again. The new church was built on what was once George Hunt's farm at the edge of Trenton Junction's original boundary, where West Upper Ferry Road and Wilburtha Road merge. Because the old church building could not be sold or repurposed, it was decided to burn the building and allow the fire department to use the event as a drill. [257]

---

[257] Michael J. Falzini. *Interview with the author.* May 12, 1991 and John "Jake" Garzio. *Interview with the author.* May 12, 1991.

CHAPTER 23

SING PRAISES

THE FOLLOWING IS A letter sent to the editor of the *Trenton Evening Times* by "J.M.A." of Trenton Junction. It was published one hundred and ten years ago, on November 12, 1906. It speaks to high quality of life in Trenton Junction both then, and now:

To the Editor of the Times:

Sir—It has been noticed recently that many towns have been boasting through the press of their many superior qualities and inducements. After observing and absorbing the good features which has been set forth, the writer of this article feels that Trenton Junction is not by any means in the background, but is rather on the alert and abreast with the march of progress in various ways.

As a residence section it is far superior to any town within a radius of fifty or more miles from Trenton, owing to its location, altitude, natural drainage, pure air and pure water, all of these being the essentials of a home. The place is just far enough away to avoid factory smoke and the general noise of a great city, and for the man with daily business in New York, Philadelphia or Trenton, it is only a matter of a short ride via the steam railroad or trolley.

The grocer, baker, milkman and butcher are in daily attendance to supply the desires of the inner man. Telephones, with the advantage of unlimited service in the Trenton circuit, are to be had at a moderate cost per year.

Public school facilities equal to city schools with promotion of pupils to the Trenton High School, at the cost of the local district, are also available.

The tax rate this year is only $1.01.

An improvement society has been organized by the broad minded men of the community for the purpose of improving conditions generally, and already many important matters have been considered and disposed of successfully, much to its credit.

A physician, with one of the most complete offices in this State, containing the most modern X-Ray and electrical equipment and generating his own power, is here.

Patients from New York, Pennsylvania and many sections of New Jersey seek treatment at this place and many cures have been recorded. Cancers have been removed entirely under this electrical treatment, while the patient suffers little or no pain. Many students have sought knowledge here.

All these conditions go far toward making an ideal home for a busy man and his family.

J.M.A.
Trenton Junction, Nov. 10, 1906

AFTERWORD

The history of Trenton Junction is a glimpse of the history of small-town, rural America as a whole. It can be argued, however, that the evolution of Trenton Junction is not typical of that small-town growth.

Trenton Junction was more than just a farming community. "At the turn of the twentieth century most Americans were farmers or came from farm families"[258] and Trenton Junction was no exception. However, in addition to the farms, there was early development of industry and mass transit.

Rural areas turned into suburbs "...when wealthy people built second homes in the country to escape the crowded, sweltering city during the summer. As roads improved...more people built summer houses."[259] Eventually, the wealthy started living outside the city full-time and commuted to work. In Trenton Junction, the railroad and trolley system made this very convenient. The development of Grand Avenue's stately homes is a direct result. Later, during the national housing shortage after World War II, more neighborhoods were formed in Ewing Township, yet Trenton Junction (by then called West Trenton) maintained its own identity.

The railroad that led to the creation of Trenton Junction allowed for its growth. In addition to allowing residents to commute to

---

[258] Alston, Julian M. Book review of "American Agriculture in the Twentieth Century: How It Flourished and What It Cost." www.eh.net/book_reviews.

[259] www.USAonline.com: "Urbanization of America."

Trenton, New York City and Philadelphia for work, it allowed industry to establish a foothold outside of those cities. If not for the railroad, there would not have been a Winner Manufacturing Company in Trenton Junction. Later, the railroad allowed other industries to come to Trenton Junction/West Trenton and Ewing: General Motors, Homasote and Roller Bearing, for example.

The airport, which started out as a grassy field and emergency landing field for the air mail system, also allowed for further growth in the area. In addition to privately owned airplanes, corporations would eventually base their aircraft there. As commercial air travel developed, the airport made it possible for commuters to travel further for work and pleasure.

It was this diversity of industry and transportation that has saved Trenton Junction (and West Trenton) from the fate faced by so many former rural communities across the country. Oftentimes, towns saw major growth based on one industry that moved into the area. Then when that industry left, the town went into decline. No so with Trenton Junction.

The links with our earliest history are still here. Yes, the appearance and sounds of Trenton Junction have changed over the years. Gone are the sounds of the farm and the factory whistle. But, the rumble of the train and roar of the airport are still here. Jones Farm and Knight Farm, though now state owned, are also reminders of our rural our past. The "West Trenton Intersection" is the same crossroads of old Birmingham that George Washington passed through on his way to the Battle of Trenton and Grand Avenue should remind us of not only the trolley and stately homes of the past, but of the Indian Trail travelled by the Lenape *sachem* who cared for the land long before the Europeans arrived.

Time has passed, but our history still surrounds us.

APPENDIX

WHAT ROAD IS THAT?

One of the most confusing aspects of studying the history of Trenton Junction is road names. Not only have entire roads had different names but even sections of the same road have been called different things at different times. There are many new roads that came into being in later years and there are some roads that were here then that are gone now. This chart will hopefully help you keep the roads straight, especially in chapter three.

West Upper Ferry Road (CR 634)
- The road that led to Green's New Ferry
- The upper Ferry Road
- Scotch Road
- Ewing Avenue

Parkway Avenue (CR 634)
- Scotch Road

Scotch Road (CR 611)
- Scotch Road

Bear Tavern Road (CR 579)
- Old River Road

Grand Avenue (CR 579)
- Old River Road

Sullivan Way (CR 579)
- Old River Road
- Asylum Road

Lower Ferry Road (CR 643)
- The Old Ferry Road

It should be noted that what is now West Upper Ferry Road used to connect not only to Parkway Avenue (as it still does today) but also with Upper Ferry Road. What is now Jack Stephen Way used to be a continuation of Upper Ferry Road into Trenton Junction. Upper Ferry Road originally crossed over Scotch Road and then made a sharp left onto today's Jack Stephen Way.

TRENTON JUNCTION
POSTMASTERS

The following is a partial listing of postmasters and their dates of appointment at the Trenton Junction Post Office, from 1882-1925:

William M. Sharp	September 21, 1882
Jonathan N. Howell	October 31, 1882
Jennie E. Howell	February 9, 1887
Theophilus Hunt	18, 1891
Lucretia Burroughs	September 12, 1891
Elizabeth Baldwin	July 12, 1894
Charles C. Lawrence	January 31, 1907
Harry Morgan	February 9, 1918
Bessie Morgan	January 8, 1920
Raymond T. Scudder	December 1, 1925

THE CENSUS

Article I Section 2 of the United States Constitution mandates that an enumeration or census be conducted every ten years to determine population distribution. This has been done every decade since 1790.

In 1920, Trenton Junction was highlighted as a special section of Ewing Township. In the column reserved for "Street Name," rather than listing the street, as was done with the rest of the township, *Trenton Junction* was inserted. Ten years later, the 1930 census for the first time segregated Trenton Junction from the rest of Ewing Township by listing it as an "unincorporated neighborhood" in the Township. No other neighborhood in the township received this distinction.[260]

The census is a treasure trove of statistical and genealogical information. From it, we can learn where people lived and who lived with them as well as their relationship to each other. Occupations are listed, as well as ages, places of origin, languages spoken, education levels and sometimes dates of immigration and naturalization. In 1930, we even learn who owned or rented their home and who owned a radio.

The Census was taken by a census taker, called the Enumerator, who went door to door and filling out the Census forms by hand. In 1920, the Enumerator was Frank H. Bukel and in 1930 the Enumerator was Grover C. Culver.

The following pages contain a statistical analysis of Trenton Junction based on the 1920 and 1930 census, followed by a listing of every Trenton Junction household and who occupied them. This provides a narrow glimpse back in time and highlights the growth and diversity inherent in the Village of Trenton Junction.

---

[260] This distinction continued in 1940, where the neighborhood is listed as "West Trenton, formerly Trenton Junction." In 1920, it should be noted, that Wilburtha was also listed separately but not in 1930.

TRENTON JUNCTION
MARCH 1920

The Fourteenth United States Census was taken in Trenton Junction during the month of March, 1920.

At this time, there were:

539 Residents (**488** if you do not include the railroad camp)

   508 residents were white
    30 residents were African-American
  164 were immigrants (**113** not including the camp)
    139 were from Italy (**88** not including camp)
     11 were from England
      3 were from Ireland
      2 were from Germany
      3 were from Hungary
      1 was from Canada
      3 were from Quebec[261]
      2 were from Lithuania

49 families owned their home. Of those, **24** were owned free and clear and **25** were mortgaged.
46 families rented their home. The status of **5** families is unknown.

15 residents were boarders.

3 residents were live-in servants

There were approximately **101** families in Trenton Junction in 1920.

---

[261] French Canadians are treated as a separate ethnic group by the United States Census Bureau.

TRENTON JUNCTION
APRIL 1930

The Fifteenth United States Census was taken in Trenton Junction during the month of April 1930.

At this time:

There were **117** dwellings; **7** were "double family" dwellings
There were **119** families (**135** if you include the families in the Railroad camp)
    16 families lived in the railroad camp
     4 families had live-in servants
     5 people living in Trenton Junction were here as live-in servants
     7 families had boarders
    19 people living in Trenton Junction were boarders
    19 people living in the railroad camp were boarders
   104 people lived in the railroad camp (**85** if you don't include the boarders)
   519 people lived in the neighborhood
   623 people lived in Trenton Junction in total

88 families owned their homes (**75%**)

83 families in Trenton Junction had radios (**71%**)

Dwellings in the railroad camp were rented for either **$13.50** or **$19.00 per month.**

The average rent in Trenton Junction was **$32.40**.

Of the **623** people living in Trenton Junction, **14** were African-American and 129 were immigrants - **20%** of the Trenton Junction population.

> **105** (**81%**) came from Italy
> > **6** from England
> > **5** from Mexico
> > **3** from Russia
> > **2** from the Irish Free State
> > **2** from Quebec
> > **2** from Canada
> > **1** from Scotland
> > **1** from Germany

BREAKDOWN BY STREET
1930

Walker Avenue

6 families

20 people

Central Avenue

4 families

19 people

Lafayette Avenue

8 families

24 people

Summit Avenue

9 families

30 people

Ewing Avenue[262]

28 families

110 people

Trenton Avenue

5 families

15 people

Washington Avenue

4 families

31 people

Carrigg Street

4 families

22 people

Hinkle Avenue

6 families

40 people

New Street

6 families

35 people

Grand Avenue

39 families

174 people

Railroad Camp

16 families

85 people

19 lodgers

104 people total

---

[262] Ewing Avenue became West Upper Ferry Road in the mid-1960s.

THE RESIDENTS OF
TRENTON JUNCTION

The following is a breakdown of Trenton Junction based on the 1930 United States Census.

The street on which each person lived is given, however house numbers were not used in 1930. Therefore it is not possible to tell the exact location of each family. Those families listed next to each other were not necessarily neighbors.

Each block represents an individual household. The first name listed is the head of the household. If female, it is usually because the woman was a widow. The name immediately listed after the head of household was usually the wife. Next are the children. If the relationship is other than son/daughter it is noted, as often times families took in boarders and lodgers and sometimes extended family members.

The occupation listed lines-up with the holder of that occupation. A blank space means that person did not have a job, either because they were retired, too young or in some cases a female, although some women did hold jobs.

The "steam railroad" was the Reading Railroad. The "electric railroad" was the local trolley.

If the individual is an immigrant, their country of origin and year of immigration is listed. For those born in the United States, the State where they were born is listed.

Street	Names	Occupation	Origin
Walker Avenue	Edith King		Ohio
	Theodore Bull (nephew)	Insurance Salesman	New York
	Helen Bull (niece)	Dry goods store saleslady	New York
	George Cutter	Mechanical (Wire rope)	Massachusetts
	Caroline Cutter		New Jersey
	Madeline Cutter		New Jersey
	Leon VanSant	Tobacco salesman	New Jersey
	Elizabeth VanSant		Pennsylvania
	Leon VanSant		New Jersey
	LeRoy VanSant		New Jersey
	Beulah P. VanSant		New Jersey
	Florence VanSant		New Jersey
	Irven VanSant	Plumber	New Jersey
	Stewart VanSant	Machinist (aircraft)	New Jersey
	William Simon	Refrigerator Painter	New Jersey
	Thelma		New Jersey
	Dolores		New Jersey
	Brian Newcomb	Carpenter	New York
	Robert Newcomb (brother)	Machinist (aircraft)	New York
			England 1872
	Sara Lewis (grandmother)		
Lafayette Avenue	John D. McCrae	Laborer	South Carolina
	Nellie		South Carolina
	Janie (sister)		South Carolina
	Peter VanTine	Painter	New Jersey
	James L. Johnson	Teacher (Deaf School)	New Jersey
	Laura P.		New Jersey
	Albert Bodine	Notions Proprietor[263]	New Jersey
	Bertha C.		New Jersey
	Jean		New Jersey

---

[263] "Notions" are small, lightweight items for household use, such as needles, thread, buttons, etc.

Street	Names	Occupation	Origin
	Mervon Fields	Bookkeeper in a cigar shop	New Jersey
	H. May		New Jersey
	Melvin J.		New Jersey
	Norman H.		New Jersey
	Donald G.		New Jersey
	George L. Hart	Credit Adjuster	New Jersey
	Beatrice A.		New Jersey
	George L. Jr.		New Jersey
	Anne Scatterweight (in-law)	Cook (private employ)	New Jersey
	Winfield L. Hart	Butcher Shop Manager	New Jersey
	Emma C.		New Jersey
	Ellard A. Buck	Public School Teacher	New Jersey
	Sue F.		New Jersey
	Robert F.		New Jersey
	Paul W.		New Jersey
Ewing Avenue[264]	Wayne C. Bleasdale	Painting Compositor	New Jersey
	Gertrude D. (mother)	Dressmaker	New Jersey
	Frederick W. (uncle)	Hat store salesman	New Jersey
	Harrold [sic] (cousin)	State Museum clerk	New Jersey
	Thomas E. Burke	Asst. Supervisor of Insurance Co.	New Jersey
	Jesse B.		New Jersey
	Thomas E. Jr.		New Jersey
	Anna K.		New Jersey
	William J.		New Jersey
	Orrien Decker	Building Contractor	New Jersey
	Anna L.		New Jersey
	Margaret J.	Stenographer - State Institution	New Jersey
	Isabel B.	Stenographer - Public School	New Jersey
	Alvin S. Brewer	Turbine "Cost Clerk"	New Jersey
	Anne C.		New Jersey
	Kenneth Fell	State Highway Bridge Detailer	New Jersey
	Frieda A.		New Jersey

---

[264] Ewing Avenue became West Upper Ferry Road in the mid-1960s.

Street	Names	Occupation	Origin
	Jeannette Wismer	Teacher at Deaf School	New Jersey
	Hanna Transuel (daughter)		New Jersey
	Emma Transuel (granddaughter)		New Jersey
	Charles Green (cousin)		New Jersey
	Joseph D. Stantial		New Jersey
	Gertrude		New Jersey
	Asenath Carey		New Jersey
	Mary Callowhill (daughter)	State Insurance Actuarial Clerk	New Jersey
	George E. Mace	Traffic Manager (Chamber of Commerce)	New Jersey
	Elizabeth		Massachusetts
Ewing Avenue	Frank H. Buchel	Vocational Experience Rehabilitator	New Jersey
	Dorothy M.		New Jersey
	Frank P.		New Jersey
	Richard L.		New Jersey
	Charles L. Zenker	Real Estate Agent	New Jersey
	Eugenia M.		New Jersey
	Sarah J. Stryker		Pennsylvania
	Charles H. Bahney	Asst. Yard Master (Wire rope)	New Jersey
	Lillian S.		Canada 1890
	Martha L.		New Jersey
	Joseph V. Hart	Dairy Truck Driver	New Jersey
	Louella		New Jersey
	Elizabeth Temple		New Jersey
			New Jersey
	George Moore (boarder)	Carpenter, Construction	New Jersey
	Emma		New York
	Charles Brook	Foreman, Brass Foundry	New Jersey
	Ella		New Jersey
	George W.	Timekeeper at Plumbing Supply	New Jersey
	Charles H. Jr.		New Jersey
	Robert B.	Asst. Foreman, Brass Foundry	New Jersey
	Margaret	Millboard Crane Operator	New Jersey
	Richard T.		New Jersey
	Mable P. (daughter-in-law)		New Jersey
	Theodore H. Ivins	Farmer	New Jersey
	Bella E.		New Jersey
	Fred	Farmer	New Jersey
	Laura Akers (sister-in-law)		New Jersey

Street	Names	Occupation	Origin
Ewing Avenue	Fred O. Lanning	Blacksmith at State Hospital	New Jersey
	Florence		New Jersey
	Wilbur S.	Payroll Clerk at Pottery	New Jersey
	Dorothy		New Jersey
	Ethel		New Jersey
	Frederick O. Jr.		New Jersey
	Elzie M. Hill	Laborer, Building Construction	Delaware
	Sarah E.		New Jersey
	Charles E.	Public School Teacher	New Jersey
	Evelyn A. Stout		New Jersey
	Joseph Schino	Laborer, Building Construction	Italy 1902
	Theresa		Italy 1906
	Pasquale		New Jersey
	Frank	Laborer, Building Construction	New Jersey
	Joseph Jr.		New Jersey
	Maraino		New Jersey
	Henry		New Jersey
	Mary R.		New Jersey
	Margaret L.		New Jersey
	Horace VanHarler	Newspaper Dealer	New Jersey
	Laura		New Jersey
	Hattie V. Stout (cousin)		New Jersey
	Seymore Hundley	Coal Truck Driver	Virginia
	Emma D.		Virginia
	Harrietta		Virginia
	Elizabeth	Servant	New Jersey
	Emma D.	Servant	New Jersey
Ewing Avenue	Frederick Fravagline	Quarry Stone Cutter	Italy 1916
	Mary		Italy 1921
	Jennie		New Jersey
	Leonard		New Jersey
	Geno		New Jersey
	Joseph		New Jersey
	Mario Rossi	Electric Trolley Track Laborer	Italy 1901
	Emilia		Italy 1917
	Rose	Laundress	New Jersey
	Philip	Water Boy - Steam RR	New Jersey
	Angelina		New Jersey
	Margaret		New Jersey
	Peter DiBlasio	Millboard Beaterman	Italy 1914
	Arina		Italy 1927
	Angelo		New Jersey

Street	Names	Occupation	Origin
	Nicola Pugliese	Electric Trolley Track Laborer	Italy 1923
	Katie		New Jersey
	Geanoto		New Jersey
	Albert DeFeo	Timekeeper - Steam RR	New Jersey
	Teresa F.		Pennsylvania
	Mario		New Jersey
	Louise (mother)		Italy 1879
	Michael Franks (boarder)	Track Laborer - Steam RR	New Jersey
	Anthony Pizzo (boarder)	Track Laborer - Steam RR	Italy 1913
	Alfred DiLeonardo (boarder)	Track Laborer - Steam RR	Italy 1923
	Jasper Walton	Produce Accountant	New Jersey
	Elizabeth M.		Pennsylvania
	Leroy J.		Pennsylvania
	Melvin L.		New Jersey
Washington Avenue	Angelo DiBlasio	Laborer, Steam RR	Italy 1912
	Anna		Italy 1914
	Viola M.	Laundress	Italy 1914
	Joseph		New Jersey
	Rose		New Jersey
	Dominick		New Jersey
	Mary		New Jersey
	Tom		New Jersey
	John		New Jersey
	Antonette		New Jersey
	Dominick DiFrancisco (Boarder)	Track Laborer - Steam RR	Italy 1914
			Italy 1913
	Nicholas Renzetti (Boarder)	Track Laborer - Steam RR	Italy 1926
	Dominick Diengenis (Boarder)	Laborer (Building)	Italy 1899
			Italy 1900
	Russell Sorodo (Boarder)	Track Laborer - Steam RR	
	Dominick DiGeorsee (Boarder)	Laborer (Building)	

Street	Names	Occupation	Origin
	Gennaro Gazillo	Track Laborer - Steam RR	Italy 1906
	Mary		Italy 1912
	Elizabeth		New Jersey
	Anna		New Jersey
	Rose		New Jersey
	Susie		New Jersey
	Luigi (boarder)	Millboard Sander	Italy 1901
	Vincent R. Gazillo	Track Laborer - Steam RR	Italy 1900
	Angelina		Italy 1927
	Frank L.		Italy 1927
Washington Avenue	Ernest Vagnozzi	Cement Maker - State Highway	Italy 1911
	Jennie		Italy 1915
	Elizabeth		New Jersey
	Antonette		New Jersey
	Elizabeth (mother)		Italy 1911
	Fannie (sister)		New Jersey
Hinkle Avenue	Luigi Carozza	Millboard Foreman	Italy 1901
	Nancy		Italy 1904
	Philip	Grocery Salesman	New Jersey
	Mary		New Jersey
	John		New Jersey
	Eleanor		New Jersey
	Elizabeth		New Jersey
	Edith		New Jersey
	Peter		New Jersey
	Joseph Croce	Millboard Sander	Italy 1895
	Mary		Italy 1900
	Guirino Miccio	Laborer - Building	Italy 1921
	Madaline	Construction	Pennsylvania
	Joseph E.		New Jersey
	Theresa M.		New Jersey
	Mary A.		New Jersey

Street	Names	Occupation	Origin
Hinkle Avenue	Vincent Schino	Millboard Pressman	Italy 1918
	Jammie		Italy 1912
	Tony	Laborer - Construction	New Jersey
	Charles		New Jersey
	Jammie		New Jersey
	Susie		New Jersey
	Dominick		New Jersey
	Rose		New Jersey
	James		New Jersey
	Paul		New Jersey
	Lucy		New Jersey
	Louis Canto	Track Laborer - Steam RR	Italy 1904
	Anna		Italy 1919
	Adam		New Jersey
	Rose		New Jersey
	John		New Jersey
	Nicholas		New Jersey
	Michael Fondette (boarder)	Track Laborer - Steam RR	Italy 1900
	Frank Dominic (boarder)		Italy 1921
		Track Laborer - Steam RR	
	Walter B. Haas	Millboard Inspector	New Jersey
	Emma		New Jersey
	Kathryn		New Jersey
	William		New Jersey
	Robert		New Jersey
Grand Avenue	Louis Garzio (widower)	Foreman, Steam RR	Italy 1907
	Nicholas	Track Laborer - Steam RR	New Jersey
	Millie		New Jersey
	John		New Jersey
	Jennie		New Jersey
	Mary		New Jersey
	Morris		New Jersey
	Albert		New Jersey
	Louis		New Jersey
	Francisco Tortello (bro-in-law)	Track Laborer - Steam RR	Italy 1901
	Edward H. Burroughs		New Jersey
	Robert Scudder	Machinist (electric)	New Jersey
	Helen		New Jersey
	E. Adella		New Jersey
	Elston		New Jersey

Street	Names	Occupation	Origin
	Frederick W. Wooley	Dairyman	New Jersey
	H. Arlean		New York
	Ruth M.		New Jersey
	Rachel Brown		England 1920
	George W. Brown	Sales manager	England 1910
	Amy M.		England 1906
	Betty M.		New Jersey
	C. John		New Jersey
	George W. Jr.		New Jersey
	Charles G. Knight	Construction Foreman	New Jersey
	Esther P.		Pennsylvania
	Phyllis		New Jersey
	Peggy Lou		New Jersey
	Gerold Curtice	Automobile Mechanic	Pennsylvania
	Lois		New Jersey
	Ross Davis	Construction Foreman	Pennsylvania
	Hattie B.		Pennsylvania
	Fred M. Staples	Accountant at State Hospital	Massachusetts
	Mary		Pennsylvania
	Marcus M.		New Jersey
Grand	Charlotte C.		New Jersey
Avenue	John E. Howell	Wallpaper Decorator	Pennsylvania
	Mary E.		New Jersey
	May Moore		New Jersey
	Anna W.	Secretary, Board of Education	New Jersey
	William Bringham	U.S. Mail Clerk	New Jersey
	Anna		New York
	Lewis	Gas-Electric Clerk	New Jersey
	Rachel (daughter-in-law)		New Jersey
	Harry D. Biles	Title Searcher for the State	New Jersey
	Helen R.	of NJ	New Jersey
	L. Wesley		New Jersey
	E. Jeane		New Jersey
	Julia D. (mother)		New Jersey

Street	Names	Occupation	Origin
Grand Avenue	Frederick Gilkyson	State Adjutant General	Pennsylvania
	Cora		New Jersey
	Charles W. Stark	Tile & Fireplace Contractor	New York
	Charles W. Jr.		New Jersey
	John Morrison	Banker	Scotland 1906
	Eleanor		New Jersey
	Laura		New Jersey
	John		New Jersey
	Elizabeth Burkhart		Pennsylvania
	Mahlon K. Neeld (brother)		Pennsylvania
	Joseph D. Mitchell		Pennsylvania
	Lucy (sister)		Pennsylvania
	Charles A. Delmonico	Millboard Blacksmith	Italy 1898
	Mary (daughter)		Italy 1914
	Amelia (daughter)		New Jersey
	Charles A. Jr. (son)		New Jersey
	Ralph Garzio	Track Laborer - Electric Trolley	Italy 1913
	Argia		Italy 1924
	Hortense		New Jersey
	Frank		Pennsylvania
	Samuel		New Jersey
	Fred L. Champion	Garage Proprietor	New Jersey
	Emily B.		New Jersey
	Celia E.		New Jersey
	Clifford B.		New Jersey
	Emily W. (adopted mother)		New Jersey
	John W. Burd	Grocery Store Proprietor	New Jersey
	Ella		New Jersey
	Lucy H.		New Jersey
			New Jersey
	Mary Corcoran (maid)	Servant	New Jersey
	Ida F. Green (nurse)	Servant	New Jersey
	Mary K. Arnold		New Jersey
	Rutherford B. (son)	Rubber Salesman	New Jersey

Street	Names	Occupation	Origin
Grand Avenue	Augustus Piccne	Millboard Finisher	Italy 1905
	Lucy		Italy 1907
	Charles		New Jersey
	Mary		New Jersey
	Juline		New Jersey
	Alevera		New Jersey
	Florence		New Jersey
	John		New Jersey
	Augustus Jr.		New Jersey
	Mary E. Paxson		New Jersey
	Rachel C. (daughter)	Stationary Saleslady	New Jersey
	Florence Kurts (daughter)		New Jersey
	Elmer J. Kurts (son-in-law)	Brakeman, Steam RR	New Jersey
	Elmer Kurts (grandson)		New Jersey
	Virginia Kurts (granddaughter)		New Jersey
	Raymond Scudder	Postmaster	New Jersey
	Annie	Grocery Proprietor	England 1898
	Elmira	Grocery Saleslady	New Jersey
	Mildred		New Jersey
	Myrtle		New Jersey
	Lester		New Jersey
Grand Avenue	Laura Woodward		Pennsylvania
	Elizabeth	Librarian, State Hospital	New Jersey
	Helen		New Jersey
	Lorelei		New Jersey
	Vincenzo Falzini	Foreman, Steam RR	Italy 1905
	Pauline		Italy 1904
	Anthony		New Jersey
	Harry		New Jersey
	Pauline		New Jersey
	Michael		New Jersey
	Teresa		New Jersey
	Ernest		New Jersey
	Mary		New Jersey
	Peter DiNicola (brother-in-law)	Pottery Molder	Italy 1916
	Edward Grover	Furniture Salesman	New Jersey
	Martha		England 1889
	Doris	Furniture Store Secretary	New Jersey
	Elva	Telegraph Semplex Operator	New Jersey
	Alma		New Jersey

Street	Names	Occupation	Origin
	John R. Scammell	Metal Lathe Salesman	Wales 1868
	John R. Jr.		New Jersey
			New Jersey
	Harriet Eldridge (housekeeper)	Servant	New Jersey
	Robert B. Gage	Chemist (State of New Jersey)	Pennsylvania
	Ita		Quebec 1915
	Lauretta		Quebec 1915
	Roberta		New Jersey
	M. Geraldine		New Jersey
	Robert B.		New Jersey
	W. Leslie Vanderpool	Public School Janitor	Wisconsin
	Mary E.		Wisconsin
	Beryl B.	Stenographer at Adj. General Office	Wisconsin
	Mena L.	Teacher at Deaf School	Nebraska
	John Y. Thackerayery	Pottery Production Clerk	New Jersey
	Jessie E.		New Jersey
	William		New Jersey
	John Y. Jr.		New Jersey
Grand Avenue	Stacy C. Smith	Dairyman	New Jersey
	Viola A.	Waitress in Restaurant	New Jersey
	James Thornton (father-in-law)		Pennsylvania
	Dominic Sebasto	Millboard Pressman	Italy 1901
	Mary R.		Italy 1906
	Nicholas		New Jersey
	Anthony	Water Boy, Steam RR	New Jersey
	Alonza		New Jersey
	Mary		New Jersey
	Michael		New Jersey
	Rose		New Jersey
	Dominic Jr.		New Jersey
	George Winkel	Dairy Proprietor	New Jersey
	Ada		New Jersey
	Sophie		New Jersey
	Lucy Ward (mother-in-law)		England 1891

Street	Names	Occupation	Origin
Grand Avenue	Joseph B. Atchley	Farmer	New Jersey
	Martha S.		Canada 1888
	Richard	Farmer	New Jersey
	M. William Howell	State Highway Roadman	Wisconsin
	Alma P.		Pennsylvania
	Virginia L.		New Jersey
	Alfred R. Jones	Dairy Manager	New Jersey
	Bertha		New Jersey
	Edwin D. Toye	Radio Salesman	Pennsylvania
	Catherine		Pennsylvania
	Oliver M. Stryker	Telephone Lineman	New Jersey
	Helen B.		New Jersey
	Eleanor C.		New Jersey
	Michael F. (father of Oliver)	Chicken Farmer	New Jersey
	Felix Liberto	Baggage Master - Steam RR	Pennsylvania
	Jessie		Italy 1920
	George		Pennsylvania
	Mary		Pennsylvania
	Frank (cousin)		Italy 1880
Central Avenue	Arthur D. McTighe	Insurance Salesman	New York
	Ruth		Massachusetts
	Donald A.		New York
	Ruth		New York
	Charlotte (mother)		New York
Central Avenue	Walter G. Sourbeer	Boiler Inspector - Steam RR	Pennsylvania
	Mary F.		Pennsylvania
	Ray C.	Dairyman	New Jersey
	William B.	Laborer	New Jersey
	Robert C.		New Jersey
	John J. Boscarelli	Lawyer	New Jersey
	Pauline M.		Pennsylvania
	John J. Jr.		New Jersey
	Oscar Lanning	Produce Proprietor	New Jersey
	Cora		New Jersey
	Donald		New Jersey
	Theodore		New Jersey
	Lucy Dey (mother-in-law)		New Jersey

Street	Names	Occupation	Origin
Summit Avenue	Marvin L. Howell Bessie C. Willing Frederick	State Highway Accountant	New Jersey Wisconsin Wisconsin New Jersey
	Charles E. Cooper Margaret C.	Insurance Salesman	New Jersey Wisconsin
	William D. Hunt Emma E. Harry M. John E. Parse (brother-in-law)	Carpenter Laboratory Worker	New Jersey New Jersey New Jersey New Jersey
	James L. Martin Emilie W. James L. Jr. Julia W.	Insurance Secretary	New Jersey New Jersey New Jersey New Jersey
	Lincoln D. Snyder Margaret	Carpenter at State Hospital	Pennsylvania Pennsylvania
Summit Avenue	William L. Healy Ethel S.	Electrical Engineer	New Jersey Pennsylvania
	Ralph G. Caldwell Effie E. Francis E. James W. Thomas S. Ralph G.	Public School Teacher	Pennsylvania Pennsylvania Pennsylvania Pennsylvania New Jersey New Jersey
	Charles E. Allen Sarah N.	Cabinet Maker	New Jersey New Jersey
	George Muirhead J. Alberta J. Ogden Muirhead Cornelia (wife)	Dairy Stock keeper Dairy Foreman	New Jersey Maryland New Jersey New Jersey
Trenton Avenue	Anthony Marocco Julia William A. Catherine M. Mary Danile Carmen DiJulia (boarder)	Track Laborer - Steam RR Track Laborer - Steam RR	Italy 1921 Italy 1921 New Jersey New Jersey New Jersey New Jersey Italy 1921

Street	Names	Occupation	Origin
	John A. Draper	Waiter at Hotel	Tennessee
	Miles Nillsouth (boarder)		Pennsylvania
	John A. Kurtz		Pennsylvania
	Mary A. Sacho (servant)		Germany (?)
Trenton Avenue	Melville Schafer	Electrician for City Police	New Jersey
	Mabel		New Jersey
	George M. Krall	Public School Teacher	Pennsylvania
	Helen H.	Public School Teacher	Pennsylvania
Carrigg Street	Francis DiFrancisco	Machinist - Steam RR	Italy 1905
	Christine		Italy 1907
	Frederick		New Jersey
	Louis (brother-in-law)	Laundry Truck Driver	Italy (?)
	Mary		New Jersey
	Dominic DiFrancisco	Fireman - Steam RR	Italy (?)
	Edith		Italy (?)
	Francisco		New Jersey
	Daniel (relative)	Track Laborer - Steam RR	Italy (?)
	Daniel (son of relative)		New Jersey
	Daniel F. Carrigg		Ireland[265] 1869
	Eugene A. (son)	Clerk - Steam RR	New Jersey
	Mary Moser (servant)		New Jersey
	John F. Carrigg	Brakeman - Steam RR	New Jersey
	Ada M.		Pennsylvania
	Edward A.		New Jersey
	Ruth E.		New Jersey
	Mary		New Jersey
Carrigg Street	John M. Tyman	Foreman - Steam RR	New Jersey[266]
	Elizabeth		New Jersey
	John	Fireman - Steam RR	New Jersey
	Francis	Crane Operator - Steam RR	New Jersey

---

[265] Irish Free State
[266] John Tyman's parents were both from the Irish Free State

Street	Names	Occupation	Origin
New Street	Georgia M. Rulon	Janitress - Steam RR	Maryland
	Asenath Cromwell (mother)		Maryland
	Joseph P. Carrigg	Stock Clerk - State Highway	New Jersey
	Josephine L.	Dept.	Pennsylvania
	Nicolo Muscente	Freightman - Steam RR	Italy 1893
	Corcetta		Italy 1893
	Anthony Muscente	Laborer - Steam RR	Italy 1900
	Mary		Italy 1920
	Pasquale		Italy 1920
	Jennie R.		Italy 1920
	Philomena		New Jersey
	Louis	Laborer - Steam RR	New Jersey
	Mary		New Jersey
	Nicholas		New Jersey
	Fred Sheferone (cousin)	Track Laborer - Electric Railroad	Italy 1912
New Street	John Ratico	Track Laborer - Steam RR	Italy 1902
	Julia		Italy 1907
	Margaret	Laundry Presser	New Jersey
	Pasquale F.		New Jersey
	Mary		New Jersey
	John Jr.		New Jersey
	Joseph		New Jersey
	Mariano		New Jersey
	Louis		New Jersey
	Ferdinando Paterra (boarder)	Stone Quarry Laborer	Italy 1922
		Track Laborer - Steam RR	Italy 1924
	Joseph Taibbi (boarder)	Track Laborer - Steam RR	Italy 1910
	John Picintino (boarder)	Foreman - Steam RR	Italy 1896
	Joseph Pasquale (boarder)		
	Ferdinando Urbano	Crane Operator - Steam Rail Road	Italy 1907
	Jennie		Italy 1922
	Nicolo		New Jersey
	Teresa		New Jersey
	Mary		New Jersey
	Philip		New Jersey
	Irma		New Jersey

Street	Names	Occupation	Origin
	Anthony Paterra	Laborer - Building	Italy 1914
	Antoinette	Construction	Italy 1920
	Damian		New Jersey
	Joseph		New Jersey
	Jennie		New Jersey
	Louise		New Jersey
	Anna		New Jersey
	Nicolo Marcucci		Italy 1914
	Consiglia	Track Laborer - Steam RR	Italy 1920
	Mary		Ohio
READING	John		Pennsylvania
RAILROAD	Ida		Pennsylvania
CAMP	Joseph		Pennsylvania
	Lucas		Pennsylvania
	Chester		Pennsylvania
	Elizabeth		Pennsylvania
	James Marino	Track Laborer - Steam RR	Italy 1902
	Mario DiStefano	Track Laborer - Steam RR	Italy 19014
	Mary D.		Italy 1923
	Angeline		Italy 1923
	Assunta		New Jersey
	Joseph		New Jersey
	Anthony		New Jersey
	Louis DiPaolo	Track Laborer - Steam RR	Italy 1913
	Columbia		New Jersey
	John		Pennsylvania
	Vito		Pennsylvania
	Mary		New Jersey
READING			
RAILROAD	Dominick Marino	Track Laborer - Steam RR	Italy 1909
CAMP	Mary		Italy 1917
	Marcella		New Jersey
	Clement		New Jersey
	Anthony		New Jersey
	Joseph		New Jersey
	Angelina		New Jersey
	Catherine		New Jersey

Street	Names	Occupation	Origin
	Gaetano Scipione	Track Laborer - Steam RR	Italy 1902
	Jovannima		Italy 1913
	Mariano Rossi	Track Laborer - Steam RR	Italy 1914
	Katie M.		Pennsylvania
	Josephine		New Jersey
	Falco		New Jersey
	Anna		New Jersey
	Paul		New Jersey
	Philomena		New Jersey
	Vincenzo Marianna (boarder)	Track Laborer - Steam RR	Italy 1925
	Lloyd T. Schneider	Painter	Wisconsin
	Rose		Pennsylvania
	Anthony Ferri	Track Laborer - Steam RR	Italy 1901
	Rose		Italy 1914
	Louis	Telegraph Operator - Steam RR	Italy 1914
	Frank	Track Laborer - Steam RR	New Jersey
	Elizabeth		New Jersey
	Joseph		New Jersey
	Pahana (?)		New Jersey
	Dominic		New Jersey
	John		New Jersey
	Nicolo		New Jersey
	Mary		New Jersey
READING RAILROAD CAMP	Dante D. Danese	Laborer - Building Construction	Italy 1911
	Margaret K.		Pennsylvania
	Peter		New Jersey
	Alfred A.		New Jersey
	Helen		New Jersey
	Angelina		New Jersey
	Mary		New Jersey
	Sabino Battista	Track Laborer - Steam RR	Italy 1909
	Mary		New Jersey
	Peter		New Jersey
	Mario		New Jersey
	Rose		New Jersey
	Louise		New Jersey
	Anna		New Jersey
	Carmela		New Jersey
	John		New Jersey
	Angelina		New Jersey
	Sabino Jr.		New Jersey

Street	Names	Occupation	Origin
	Giampietro DiGiovocchino	Track Laborer - Steam RR	Italy 1907
	Helen		Italy 1910
	Vincenzo	Truck Driver for Stone Quarry	Italy 1918
	Marli		New Jersey
	Andrew	Track Laborer - Steam RR	New Jersey
	Charles	Water Boy - Steam RR	New Jersey
READING RAILROAD CAMP	Pio Tisschio	Track Laborer - Steam RR	Italy 1913
	George Barclay (lodger)	Track Laborer - Steam RR	Pennsylvania
	Michael Jadach (lodger)	Track Laborer - Steam RR	Poland 1913
	Charles Morris (lodger)	Track Laborer - Steam RR	Pennsylvania
	Edward Gallop (lodger)	Track Laborer - Steam RR	Pennsylvania
	Harry Opfer (lodger)	Track Laborer - Steam RR	Pennsylvania
	Robert McNichol (lodger)	Track Laborer - Steam RR	Pennsylvania
	Frank Carr (lodger)	Track Laborer - Steam RR	Pennsylvania
	Anthony Lantz (lodger)	Track Laborer - Steam RR	Russia 1913
	Patrick Thompson (lodger)	Track Laborer - Steam RR	Ireland[267] 1913
	Nicholas Babitch (lodger)	Track Laborer - Steam RR	Russia 1913
	Daniel Zace	Track Laborer - Steam RR	Russia 1912
	Edward Maloney	Track Laborer - Steam RR	Massachusetts
	Huger Mullen (lodger)	Track Laborer - Steam RR	Pennsylvania
	James McWilliams (lodger)	Track Laborer - Steam RR	Pennsylvania
	Patrick Tahney (lodger)	Track Laborer - Steam RR	Pennsylvania
READING RAILROAD CAMP	Augustin Rosales	Track Laborer - Steam RR	Mexico 1923
	Raul Garcia (lodger)	Track Laborer - Steam RR	Mexico 1920
	Dolores Marmda (lodger)	Track Laborer - Steam RR	Mexico 1920
	Marcdano Zamarpa (lodger)	Track Laborer - Steam RR	Mexico 1920
	Jesus Perez (lodger)	Track Laborer - Steam RR	Mexico 1914

---

[267] Ireland Free State

NEWSPAPERS

The following is a list of newspapers consulted and cited throughout this book. Each one contained at least one article pertaining to Trenton Junction.

Newspaper	Location
Allentown Leader	Allentown, Pennsylvania
Altoona Tribune	Altoona, Pennsylvania
Asbury Park Press	Asbury Park, New Jersey
Atlanta Constitution	Atlanta, Georgia
Belvidere Standard	Belvidere, Illinois
Bismarck Tribune	Bismarck, North Dakota
Bremen Enquirer	Bremen, Indiana
Bristol Daily Courier	Bristol, Pennsylvania
Brooklyn Daily Eagle	Brooklyn, New York
Bucks County Gazette	Bristol, Pennsylvania
Capital Times	Madison, Wisconsin
Charlotte News	Charlotte, North Carolina
Chatham Press	Chatham, New Jersey
Decatur Herald	Decatur, Illinois
Democrat & Chronicle	Rochester, New York
Democratic Banner	Mount Vernon, Ohio
El Paso Herald	El Paso, Texas
Evening Democrat	Warren, Pennsylvania
Evening Journal	Wilmington, Delaware
Evening News	Harrisburg, Pennsylvania
Evening Report	Lebanon, Pennsylvania
Evening Times	Sayre, Pennsylvania
Evening True American	Trenton, New Jersey
Evening World	New York, New York
Ft. Wayne Daily News	Ft. Wayne, Indiana
Gettysburg Times	Gettysburg, Pennsylvania
Goldsboro Headlight	Goldsboro, North Carolina
Harrisburg Daily Independent	Harrisburg, Pennsylvania

Newspaper	Location
Harrisburg Telegraph	Harrisburg, Pennsylvania
Hopewell Herald	Hopewell, New Jersey
Indianapolis Star	Indianapolis, Indiana
Junction City Union	Junction City, Kansas
Kingsport Times	Kingsport, Tennessee
Lebanon Courier & Semi-Weekly	Lebanon, Pennsylvania
Lebanon Daily News	Lebanon, Pennsylvania
Lincoln Evening Journal	Lincoln, Nebraska
Los Angeles Herald	Los Angeles, California
Los Angeles Times	Los Angeles, California
Middletown Times Herald	Middletown, New York
Montrose Democrat	Montrose, Pennsylvania
Morning Herald	Hagerstown, Maryland
Morning News	Wilmington, Delaware
Mount Caramel Item	Mount Caramel, Pennsylvania
Muskogee Times-Democrat	Muskogee, Oklahoma
New York Times	New York, New York
New-York Tribune	New York, New York
Ottawa Daily Republic	Ottawa, Kansas
Pittsburgh Daily Headlight	Pittsburgh, Kansas
Pittston Gazette	Pittston, Pennsylvania
Portsmouth Herald	Portsmouth, New Hampshire
Post-Crescent	Appleton, Wisconsin
Raleigh Times	Raleigh, North Carolina
Reading Times	Reading, Pennsylvania
Reno Gazette-Journal	Reno, Nevada
Scranton Republican	Scranton, Pennsylvania
Steuben Republican	Angola, Indiana
Tennessean	Nashville, Tennessee
The Citizen	Berea, Kentucky
The News	Frederick, Maryland
The Sun	New York, New York
The Times	Philadelphia, Pennsylvania
Topeka State Journal	Topeka, Kansas

Newspaper	Location
Trenton Evening Times	Trenton, New Jersey
Trenton Sunday Times Advertiser	Trenton, New Jersey
Trenton Times	Trenton, New Jersey
Vicksburg Evening Post	Vicksburg, Mississippi
Washington Times	Washington, DC
Wilkes-Barre Record	Wilkes-Barre, Pennsylvania
Wilkes-Barre Times Leader	Wilkes-Barre, Pennsylvania
Williamsport Sun-Gazette	Williamsport, Pennsylvania
Winston-Salem Journal	Winston-Salem, North Carolina
York Daily	York, Pennsylvania

60420572R00123

Made in the USA
Middletown, DE
29 December 2017